Praise for Christine Comaford
and the SmartTribes Institute (STI)

"Christine is super-high bandwidth."
—Bill Gates

"Christine's leadership tools are some of the most effective ones I have seen for quite some time. The neuroscience-based approach is very new and very powerful. It has made a big difference for our folks, particularly in the areas of fostering collaboration (by helping people better understand the needs and moods of their teammates) and increasing productivity (by helping our managers focus and tell apart the high-value-added activities from the low-value-added ones). These tools are easy to reapply to many different business situations and are especially useful in fast-changing business environments."
—Alberto Moriana, Head of Sales Latin America,
Procter & Gamble

"We've really moved the needle in our first year with STI! From our initial work at our Sales and Marketing Intensive and from coaching thereafter, together we've secured a needle-moving eight-digit account using two of the strategies I created with Christine and our team. This is a top three account for us. We have also doubled our marketing message effectiveness and increased our profile and brand awareness in the marketplace significantly; we've doubled our response rate on outbound marketing communications; we've created a scalable sales and marketing foundation to support our projected growth; we've launched an omni-channel marketing approach that is delivering double-digit response rates; we've developed a content marketing strategy and social media presence that is engaging prospects and clients at new levels; and we've just received the largest inbound lead in company history!

"Working with STI is efficient, effective, and high on ROI. STI brings a proven set of best practices to the table that streamlines the sales

and marketing process and delivers results. If you want to take your sales and marketing to the next level, you'll want them on your team."
—Scott Patsiga, President, Telaid

"STI's Building Brilliant Teams training is a key course in our leadership development program. Our leaders like the high interactivity, the hands-on labs, and the practical brain-based tools that are easy to learn and immediately create high-impact results. The case studies that help clarify STI's key tools are popular too. Our leaders especially like learning how to tie the neuroscience and emotional drivers of satisfaction and motivation to drive team performance and happiness. It's called 'a great class and one of the best I've attended!' by many.

"Thanks, STI, for helping us invest in leadership growth. As a result, our leaders are raising the bar on building brilliant teams."
—Steve Degnan, Chief HR Officer,
Nestlé Purina PetCare North America

"Christine received the top rating at our Fortune Leadership Summit. Her program on building trust in tangible, measurable, specific ways by showing us how it is experienced in the brain was life changing. Our audience of 650 business leaders was captivated by her message and engaged as we did labs together to apply Christine's neuroscience-based tools. It's been over a month, and our participants keep raving about it! We can't wait to work with Christine again."
—Verne Harnish, Chair, *Fortune* Magazine's Leadership
Summit, and author of *Scaling Up*

"I've been in the sales and marketing world for decades, and I can be a bit skeptical of consultants. Christine changed all that. From the start she was generous with her time, ROI focused, and profoundly accountable.

"The results have been amazing. In two workshops, Christine's potent neuroscience techniques have completely refreshed how our marketing leadership team approaches messaging, customer experience, optimizing our marketing process, and aligning with sales. Our team has called the experience nothing short of amazing—and we're not known to gush. Thanks, STI!"
—Steve Mann, former CMO, LexisNexis

"The program we had recently with STI was one of the highest rated of the year! Christine did prework to learn what our members' top business challenges were, and then she brought exactly what we needed to solve them. She made sure we understood how to use the tools, she gave us specifics on applying them to different scenarios, and she also was very generous with extra tools and extra time. The whole day was nonstop take-home value! Our members didn't know it was possible to get this much value in a single program. We will definitely have Christine work with our CEOs again. Everyone gave overwhelmingly positive feedback!"

—Daniel Levin, CEO, Cain Millwork, and
Education Chair, YPO Chicago

"Our sincerest thanks for your fantastic work at our summit. Your energy is amazing, your expertise beyond valuable, and the STI team is wonderful to work with! Our leaders found the day to be packed with practical tools they could immediately apply to help their teams rise to new levels of engagement, performance, and connection. In times of change and growth, your powerful yet easy brain-based tools are already making a difference for our tribe. We can't wait to work together further."

—Tim Herrod, Vice President Procurement,
Potash Corporation

"Thank you so much, Christine, for the brilliance, passion, and inspiration you've imprinted on the mind and heart of each of us. Your program at our first GoPro Women's Summit empowered everyone profoundly. We have received so much incredible feedback from our attendees! Now they have new tools to help them generate new insights and help others do the same, to make new meaning about their experiences, to bring safety, belonging, and mattering where it is needed so they can lead themselves, others, and the business with a fresh perspective. We can't thank you enough for leading such an impactful session. Your brain-based tools are truly helping our tribe!"

—Laura Robblee, Senior Director, GoPro

"Our event with Christine was one of our best ever! The roomful of 100+ leaders was fully engaged for an entire day. I've never seen anything like it. Christine took the time to learn what would benefit our members most, and then she designed a custom program that blew everyone's mind. The tools were just what we needed to take our teams to the next level, to create deeply engaging company cultures, to market more effectively, and to close sales faster. We're all high performers, and it's rare that we hear something that fascinates us. Christine's program had everyone diving in, learning new techniques, applying them to key business challenges, and buzzing about how they could share these tools with their teams. What a remarkable session! We'll have Christine here again."

—Scott Stevenson, President and CEO, Kleenmark, and
Education Chair, YPO Wisconsin

"What is empowerment, really? We wanted to bring our amazing team to the next level, and STI is helping us do just that. First, it had to start with me. Through coaching, I'm learning to let go more, and I have optimized my time to do more strategic (and fulfilling) work and, most important, to have more time with my family. I am no longer focused on how activities are getting accomplished down in the weeds. Instead, I am enjoying the benefits of having a strategic focus and determining the direction the organization is headed. The one-on-one attention that STI has given me and the key members of my executive management team is the reason we are becoming a more strategic and aligned organization.

"As a result, together we're continuously surpassing revenue goals and getting increasingly comfortable with even loftier revenue targets; achieving new highs in production; diversifying our client base while getting closer to and more involved in our key clients' businesses; gaining visibility on the business and having a lot less stress; helping the team across the entire organization perform at greater levels with deeper fulfilment; and receiving a Best Places to Work award based on voting by our employees.

"Now I really know what empowerment is. Our people live it, and so do I."

—Brandon Ewing,
CEO, Server Technology

"In today's world of constant change, leaders need simple and powerful tools to support their teams. STI's practical, evidence-based tools that you introduced to our sales and underwriting managers were met with appreciation and excitement. You delivered the workshop in a way that connected with our emotions and intellect. I'm confident that the tools will help us focus on critical objectives and keep our energy high. We found our time together to be of high value."

—Dennis Lum, VP National Channel Strategy,
Kaiser Permanente

"Our first year working with STI has been better than I ever imagined. It's as if our whole team has risen to an entirely new level. It's awesome and energizing! The results we're getting as a result of our work with STI are tangible too.

"Together we've created a compelling mission, vision, values, and company theme statements everyone loves; cultural rituals for engagement (high fives, celebrations and/or rewards for modeling our values); performance motivation, measurement, and growth processes (self-evaluations, leader reviews, individual development plans, personal improvement processes); accountability structures and tracking systems; three-year strategic plans with specific tactics, dependencies, and contingencies to ensure execution; three-year budget and staffing plans; a five-year map to our next key inflection point.

"I knew our team was remarkable, but seeing them dive into greater depths of leadership, enrolling and engaging others, collaborating in new and powerful ways, embracing new skills, and helping to cultivate and elevate others has been a profoundly fulfilling experience. Thanks, STI, for helping us step into our huge potential!"

—Chris Whitney, CEO, Trans-Phos, YPO Tampa

"As a finance executive, it's key to make sure that you're seen for the strategic value you bring. That's one of the many reasons coaching with STI has been so transformative. I've significantly increased my ability to deliver strategic value across our organization by raising the bar as a leader. I'm now more present with others, listening more deeply, sharing my vision more clearly, and enrolling and engaging people like never before. As a result, I've built more powerful connections and greater trust with senior executives, peers, and team members—all of which is crucial as our business continues to grow, change, and evolve.

"My team is responding too. We're more cohesive, effective, energized, and on point than ever before. My relationships are richer and closer with more open communication. Together, we're achieving more, influencing more, and seeing conflicts and challenges as exciting adventures. I'm now someone who powerfully and quickly brings people together and delivers results that far exceed expectations. I'm now seen as a strategic asset, a trusted advisor, and a cultivator of talent and people in general. Thanks, STI!"

—Michael Trzupek, former General Manager Venture
Integration Strategic Programs, Microsoft

"I've been to some of the top business growth programs in the country, and I've found STI's methodology to be among the most effective. The positive transformation our company has experienced with STI has been profound.

"Here are some of our results from strategy days, trainings, and executive coaching sessions with STI: We've powerfully aligned our geographically distributed leadership team with clear communication, needle movers, performance expectations, and proven processes to streamline results and save everyone time and energy. We've defined compelling values that everyone is rallying around, and our associate engagement continues to climb. We've created Customer Journeys, Safety, Belonging, and Mattering (SBM) Triggers, and Meta Program Profiles for our top five customer profiles. Now we know how to step into their shoes and connect more deeply with them and provide even greater service, communication, and joy in working with us.

"We've raised the bar on our already high standards of performance, service, and behavior with programs our associates have created. The company's infrastructure is in place now, and it is evolving to support our rapid growth. We're reaching new revenue and customer delight records, and we have high visibility on our finances and operations overall.

"As a result, it's now easier to recruit new associates—to onboard them and to bring them powerfully into our high-performing tribe. What a difference STI's proven processes make! Thanks, STI, for helping us reach new heights (and have fun in the process)!"

—Abigail Kampmann, CEO, Principle Auto Group,
YPO San Antonio

"Wow—our team had several aha moments at our recent Sales and Marketing Intensive with Christine. Now we clearly see what we're not doing, what we can be doing, and how exactly to do it to get the increased results we want. Christine helped us fill in the gaps to streamline sales and marketing processes, identify the profiles (and surprising similarities) of our diverse prospects, launch powerful neuroscience-based messaging for a new service, and further align our sales and marketing teams around common objectives—all while laying out a clear path. Our team is jazzed—it's as if the lights have been turned on bright and we can see farther and with greater detail.

"If you want to jumpstart your sales and marketing and get better results with a lot less effort, bring STI in to help. Your team, like mine, will thank you, and you'll love the results."

—John Gorski, CEO, NAMSA, YPO Maumee Valley

"Christine's session at our chapter was our best so far! Everyone stayed well past the ending time, and the comments on the tremendous take-home value continue to stream in. Her expertise in applied neuroscience is vast—she taught us techniques for optimizing sales, marketing, leadership, and execution, and she explained them in easy-to-learn and powerful ways. Christine was generous with her time, working one-on-one with chapter members and even with our forum to iron out key leadership challenges. It was a truly invigorating event!"

—Luke Williams, Managing Director,
Oak Tree Development, and Education Chair,
YPO Connecticut

"Our first year with STI has been a total game changer! Emotional engagement is our highest ever: we're all super aligned behind a vision we share, and we are totally in sync. Communication is also at an all-time high: we're open, compassionate, clear, and honest with each other, and we now have new levels of collaboration and trust. The results have been tangible, measurable, and specific: new clients, increased operational efficiency, some of the best work we've ever created, and it feels like we're just beginning to hit our stride.

"Thank you for helping us raise our level of leadership, for helping us optimize our culture and org chart, for helping us set clear and compelling needle movers, and so much more. Our marketing is more effective than ever before, our updated values, mission, and vision are inspiring everyone, and our new tools to increase engagement, communication, and prioritization are taking us to new heights. Wow. I knew our team was awesome, and they just keep raising the bar. I'm so glad we're on this adventure together!"

—Cheryl Farr, Founder, SIGNAL.csk Brand Partners

"When CEOs spend a full day learning about leadership, the expectations are sky high. And Smart Tribes Institute delivered! Christine's session for the Silicon Valley Chapter was one of the strongest workshops we've had. Christine helped us understand the basics of the human brain. We learned about STI's easy and potent tools to enroll, engage, align, and empower our teams in immediate and high-impact ways. As leaders, the labs we did during the workshop helped us address our real-world challenges and apply STI's tools to them. Everyone is still buzzing about the program. We can't wait to have her back!"

—Nancy Geenen, Silicon Valley Chapter Chair,
Women President's Organization

"What a high impact day at our recent Sales & Marketing Intensive! Lots of great feedback from our team. VERY impactful for us. I was thrilled by how quickly everyone grasped your powerful brain-based rapport tools.

Our team is fired up and charging ahead at remarkable speed. They are already working on direct mail concepts using their new rapport tools—they'll present them in two weeks. Our infographics are being optimized for high response rates with Safety, Belonging, Mattering, Meta Programs, WIIFM, CURVE, and the four Customer Journey Personas we created together are ready for validation. Our Sales and Marketing Needle Movers are clear and all our programs are tied directly to them, and our new marketing plan has been shared and all are engaged, aligned, enrolled. The Sales team is on board with the new stages, probabilities, and X Factor to streamline pipeline visibility and performance. Our client success stories are teed up and will be deployed easily, ensuring we amplify the awesome work our organization does for our clients.

"We now have the tools to support our Sales and Marketing team members to bring their personal best every single day.

"Our day together was the most productive and high ROI sales/ marketing gathering I've ever experienced. And I've experienced plenty of them! Thank you, Christine and STI! I can't wait to see what we create together next."

—Patrick Gallagher , Vice President, Gallagher Asphalt
Corporation, YPO Chicago

POWER
your
TRIBE

POWER your TRIBE

create resilient teams in turbulent times

CHRISTINE COMAFORD

Mc
Graw
Hill
Education

NEW YORK CHICAGO SAN FRANCISCO ATHENS
LONDON MADRID MEXICO CITY MILAN
NEW DELHI SINGAPORE SYDNEY TORONTO

1 2 3 4 5 6 7 8 9   LHN   22 21 20 19 18 17

ISBN: 978-1-260-10877-4
MHID: 1-260-10877-5

eISBN: 978-1-260-10878-1
eMHID: 1-260-10878-3

Disclaimer: The Publisher and the Author make no representations or warranties with respect to the accuracy or completeness of the contents of this work and specifically disclaim all warranties, including without limitation warranties of fitness for a particular purpose. No warranty may be created or extended by sales or promotional materials. The advice and strategies contained herein may not be suitable for every situation. This work is sold with the understanding that the Publisher is not engaged in rendering legal, accounting, or other professional services. If professional assistance is required, the services of a competent professional person should be sought. Neither the Publisher nor the Author shall be liable for damages arising herefrom. The fact that an organization or website is referred to in this work as a citation and/or a potential source of further information does not mean that the Author or the Publisher endorses the information the organization or website may provide or recommendations it may make. Further, readers should be aware that Internet websites listed in this work may have changed or disappeared between when this work was written and when it is read. In order to protect client confidentiality, all case studies in this book either are amalgamations of multiple companies and/or have had the organization's industry and possibly the gender of the executives mentioned altered. In the unusual event that sources were not cited, please notify the author via www.SmartTribesInstitute.com.

McGraw-Hill Education books are available at special quantity discounts to use as premiums and sales promotions or for use in corporate training programs. To contact a representative, please visit the Contact Us page at www.mhprofessional.com.

*To every person
on this gorgeous and mysterious planet.
May you feel safe.
May you feel you belong.
May you feel you matter.
Thanks for being here.
We're all so glad you are.*

*To my remarkable husband, Geoff Heron,
who inspires me to love more deeply every single day.*

*And to Spike,
who was born emotionally resilient.*

Contents

Foreword

As an expert in behavioral change, I find *Power Your Tribe: Create Resilient Teams in Turbulent Times* by Christine Comaford to be a fascinating exploration of the importance of managing and navigating our emotions to our personal success and to our success in working together in teams. Though I am certainly not an expert in emotional intelligence the way Christine is, our approaches to change are similar. We both target and isolate areas where change can happen and then tell you how you can make the modifications you need to achieve the results you want for yourselves and your teams.

For example, one of my favorite parts of *Power Your Tribe* is Christine's discussion of "resistance." She writes, "Resistance stabilizes the Present State, which is where the problem is. Learn how to release resistance so you can be more agile and have more choices." With this eloquently stated premise, Christine then walks us through just exactly how to release resistance so that we will have those choices. She defines the problem (with an example), explores the promise (the outcome of working with this process), and then describes the result of the efforts made in a matter-of-fact, research- and case study–based, easy-to-read account that will change your life and the lives of those around you.

Power Your Tribe is an exceptionally well written book that you will want to take chapter by chapter, line by line, tool by tool and practice both by yourself and with your teams. I highly recommend that you learn all you can from this book, implement that learning in your workplace, and let it take you to and keep you at the heights of emotional agility and success!

Life is good.

—Marshall Goldsmith
Thinkers50 #1 Leadership Thinker in the World

Preface

A Fortune 500 consumer products organization was facing a crisis—5,000 people in their Latin America sales and marketing division were in Critter State (fight, flight, freeze, or faint). With unstable and plunging currencies, unpredictable dictators, and supply chains that disappeared overnight, Latin America was the worst-performing region. Change was a constant, crisis was the result, and no one knew when the next disaster would strike. Executive leadership reached out to us, asking our help to get its 5,000 struggling people into their Smart State (where they could more easily navigate change and reduce stress).

We started with 50 leaders, teaching them our proven and easy neuroscience-based tools in an intensive daylong session. With greater emotional agility, they experienced rapid progress and told their colleagues. Then we worked with the next batch of 50, and so on, until the top 200 leaders and executors were on board. People stopped seeing themselves as victims and started seeing themselves as outcome creators. Their only question was, "What outcome do we want to create today?"

The empowerment spread outward, downward, and upward, across the organization. And two and a half years later, Latin America was the top performer—delivering over 50 percent of the growth annually to the entire corporation. Our client's executives knew their people had the power within themselves to triumph. They simply needed some new tools.

• • •

A U.S.-based healthcare provider faced a different type of change challenge: the extreme stress that comes with exponential growth. The leaders had nearly doubled the size of their organization from $13 billion to over $20 billion from their acquisition of a key competitor. The finance team had a tremendous task before it: how to integrate both companies, streamline financial operations, reduce redundancies, navigate politics, and sidestep sacred cows, all while honoring the "nice" culture our client was famous for. The finance leaders were overworked, their teams were super stressed, and the work was just beginning.

We started with a yearlong program to boost leadership and deeply empower the finance leaders to "move the decision-making down" that had historically been held closely in the C suite. As the leaders embraced our neuroscience-based tools, they cultivated and elevated their teams, stopped giving orders (and started asking questions), and transformed the change experience from fear and uncertainty into empowerment and ownership. In six months the team was emotionally agile, self-directed, and firing on all cylinders.

• • •

A market-leading food organization was in a bind. A fake news story on social media had spread like wildfire, and revenues of one of their top brands had plunged 27 percent. It was crucial to stop the slide, stabilize, and then start to rebuild.

We were brought in to train a few dozen leaders in optimal teaming, rapidly engaging and enrolling large and diverse groups to come together, focus on outcomes, tell themselves and each other new stories about their situation, and get momentum going. Then we shifted our focus to the marketing team, supporting an initiative to reinvent how the organization marketed to consumers. We started the day with an intense emotion-shifting exercise. Fifteen minutes into it, half the team had shifted from victimhood and disaster thinking to empowerment and possibility thinking. Fifteen more minutes, and the other half were on board. Now it was time to teach them how to bring our tools to their teams.

The result: The brand is safe and growing, and the leaders are stepping into new levels of accountability, meaning, and fulfillment—and they are bringing their teams forward with them. If a disaster ever strikes again, they'll navigate it gracefully and swiftly.

• • •

These very different companies have three things in common. First, they all have faced the challenges of constant, relentless, and unpredictable change. And they're only going to see more of that in today's super-fast, information-overloaded, immediate-response world.

Second, they have the driving need to shift their panicking teams to a more resourceful state in which they are *emotionally agile*—and to mobilize these teams quickly and efficiently toward a clear outcome. Knowing what you need to do and how to get to where you want is not sufficient. People—including you as the leader—must be trained, equipped, and capable of taking the necessary action to shift their *emotional* state in order to get there.

Third, when these companies used the SmartTribes tools to become more emotionally agile, they began to succeed at speeds most companies struggle to achieve.[1] Constant, relentless change was now an opportunity to *grow*, not just "go."

In other words, all these companies needed to get people on board to create necessary change. It wasn't a choice. It was a necessity. All needed new tools because the ones that had worked in the past were no longer effective. They needed a new way to *power their tribes*.

Power Your Tribe is the next evolution and extension of our *New York Times*–bestselling book *SmartTribes*.[2] Though it is worth your time to read *SmartTribes* at some stage, you don't need to read it to benefit from this book.

If you *have* read *SmartTribes*, *Power Your Tribe* reinforces the core principles you are familiar with and provides new tools. As the business environment has changed significantly in recent years—making it even clearer that relentless change is now the norm—we at SmartTribes Institute (STI) are continually discovering, pioneering, and implementing new frames of operation and behavior. We do this to support our clients who are faced with—and will continue to be faced with—change.

Where *SmartTribes* explained how teams become brilliant together, *Power Your Tribe* shows how teams use emotional agility to *stay* brilliant together—no matter how turbulent the times and no matter what external changes you face.

WHERE CHANGE OCCURS

Change appears in many forms, including these:

- External threats, in which people feel victimized by constant change from both external forces and senior leadership's response to those forces

- Exciting and often significant external and/or internal opportunities for growth

- Internal changes in structure, administration, leadership, or policies

Resistance to change is often due to the uncertainty about what it means or what may result from it. And it is important to understand that change occurs on many levels, including environment, behavior, capability, belief, identity, and core, which you'll learn more about in Chapter 1.

Changes in any of these areas are tremendously threatening to our reptilian brain, which exists to ensure that we survive. Because our reptilian brain thinks change just might kill us, it can subconsciously keep us from making the change we know we need—as you'll see in Chapter 2.

One of the greatest challenge that come with change is the feeling of isolation, fear, uncertainty, and doubt. When we're unsure of how to move forward and unclear about what the change means, we often withdraw and isolate ourselves to make sense of what is happening. But we are tribal beings. We need to be together. We need to know we're safe, we belong, and we matter.

So the key to successful change is understanding and navigating the *emotional* undercurrent of change *together*. Where other approaches deal with the surface issues involved in change, in this book we'll dive deeply into the emotional undertow that often accompanies growth and change so you can learn how to remove emotional resistance to get where you need to be.

This is not to be confused with *removing* your emotions, ignoring them, or setting them aside. This book is about learning how to *use* emotions to win. You will learn first how to shift your own emotional state and then how to shift the emotional state of others—and pursue the outcomes you want together. Because while we can't control external events, we can absolutely control our *internal* events—how we respond to all that is happening outside of us (and even inside of us).

CHANGE AND GROWTH REQUIRE EMOTIONAL AGILITY

What if I told you that a bird doesn't need its wings to fly from *A* to *B*? Or that it doesn't need to flap its wings to fly? You'd think I was being preposterous.

Wings for a bird are like emotions for human beings. Life is an emotional experience. Work is an emotional experience. Human beings *navigate* with their emotions. Emotions are the wings that get us from *A* to *B*. Without them, we can't fly. The greatest highs, lows, triumphs, and fears all come from emotional experience. Emotions are a large part of how we experience the world, each other, and ourselves. And *emotional agility* is how well we use our wings to fly.

Daniel Goleman's groundbreaking book *Emotional Intelligence* changed the way we think about human interaction—and made it OK to acknowledge that humans are emotional beings, even at work.[3] The concept of emotional intelligence is crucial for us all to understand because the lack of it causes the majority of human conflicts, including terminations, divorces, and even wars.

But as most of us realize, it's not enough to simply *know* that emotional intelligence is important. Whereas emotional intelligence informs us about the quality of our wings, *Power Your Tribe* will teach you *how* to use those wings to great effect. In a sense, this book picks up where *Emotional Intelligence* leaves off—it reveals how to change your behavior at the subconscious level to increase your emotional intelligence.

But how *do* we shift our emotional state to achieve the outcomes we want, especially when we're overwhelmed by constant change? We certainly know it's not as simple as telling ourselves, "OK, let's look at this in a positive light." Nor is it useful to tell someone, "Stop feeling overwhelmed. It's not helping anybody!"

There are *steps* to changing our emotional state. The first thing we need to know is that it's not what happens to us that matters. It's the meaning we attach to what happens that matters. And the meaning we attach is based on what we tell ourselves about what happened. If what we tell ourselves is positive, we'll have good feelings. If what we tell ourselves is negative, we'll have bad feelings. If it feels good, we'll call it a good experience. If it feels bad, we'll call it a bad experience.

However, the meaning we make about what happens to us often operates well outside our conscious awareness. It not only governs how we behave, it can also limit our capabilities—which is why it's essential to understand the meaning we are making so we can change it if need be.

According to *neuro-linguistic programming* (NLP), the human organism will always move toward the best *kinesthetic feeling*, which is the feeling or emotion we associate with a given experience (that is, the meaning we give it). In neurolinguistic shorthand, it's known as the "best K." If there isn't a best K, it will move toward the *least bad* K. And since we'll keep experiencing what we're experiencing until we're done with it, it's important to be present in what is truly happening—and to clarify the meaning, find out what the Ks are, fully appreciate them, cease resisting, and create a vision for what we want next.

Let me give you an example. Suppose you're a sales director, and a big client—one that accounts for 30 percent of your top-line revenue—stops working with you. Now you need to either replace that client or let go of some staff, maybe delay mission-critical initiatives, and explain the loss to the board. It feels bad, so it *is* bad. And you, as the sales director, may want to avoid feeling bad at all costs, whether that be via denial, avoidance, freezing up, or resolving to take your anger and frustration out on your team, all of which probably will create an environment of blame instead of collaboration.

However, avoiding bad feelings comes at a cost too. An opportunity cost. A more emotionally agile sales director might still feel bad about losing a big client. It would be strange if she didn't. But the more emotionally agile sales director will also have another feeling available to her—the feeling of inspiration that comes with the challenge. Thus, that sales director will behave differently. She will consider it an opportunity to speak to the lost client and clarify with specificity *why* that client left. Rather than using the negative feelings as a sign of failure, she'll relate to those feelings as feedback and an impetus for growth. She might redirect her attention to incorporating the feedback from the lost client and mobilize the team to plug the holes in the company's main service offering so that the rest of the client base won't suffer the same consequences.

This agile maneuver can result in increased penetration per client and increased top-line revenue per client account. The difference that made the difference? The *meaning* that the sales director made and the *feelings* that were available to her as a result.

If we want to inspire a new behavior in people to achieve better results, then we need to create a better K around what we want those people (or ourselves) to do versus the pattern they (or we) keep repeating, which currently has the best K (or least bad K). As leaders, it's our job to add more options to the menu of possible behaviors—both for others and for ourselves. This is one of the key tools you'll be learning in this book.

Experience *can* be changed. We do this by changing what we tell ourselves about our experiences (the meaning we make), which changes how we feel and changes how we classify the experience. And yes, at times, we will help others change what they tell themselves. Because another job of leaders is to help expand the identities of their people: to help them see how much choice and power they truly have.

Emotional agility is, in essence, about choosing how you want to feel, and helping others choose how they feel too. If emotions are the muscle, then emotional agility is the flexibility, strength, and adaptability of the muscle. With the right tools and the right training, this form of agility can be built into the *muscle memory* of your organization. And the more emotionally agile your organization becomes, the less it will need to "think" about becoming more agile. What would that mean for your organization?

YOUR PLAYBOOK FOR CHANGE

Power Your Tribe is based on the STI methodology we have created over the last 30-plus years of helping leaders get the results they want in organizations ranging from startups through Fortune 10 multinationals. Our blend of mapping diverse neuroscience research to practical tools and techniques has generated the many results our clients rave about.

In this book, you're going to learn how to build emotional agility through a process called the *Resilience Cycle*, which follows the change progression we see most commonly (Figure P.1).

We generally start out either *resisting* change or feeling annoyed and/or frustrated by it. Here most of us stay stuck, refusing to see change for what it is—an opportunity to acknowledge that what worked before doesn't any longer or that the conditions in our life are now new.

Once we are able to move through resistance, we can stay present to what's happening by *increasing rapport with ourselves*. As a result, we can *create new meaning, expand our identity*, and ultimately have more choices. Then, with new choices open to us, we can *anchor the outcome* we want, *enroll and engage* our tribe in pursuing that outcome, and keep everyone *agile* and *powerful* as new changes arise.

Note: You may pop into the process at any point in the cycle. For example, if you're not resisting anything but need to make new meaning, start there.

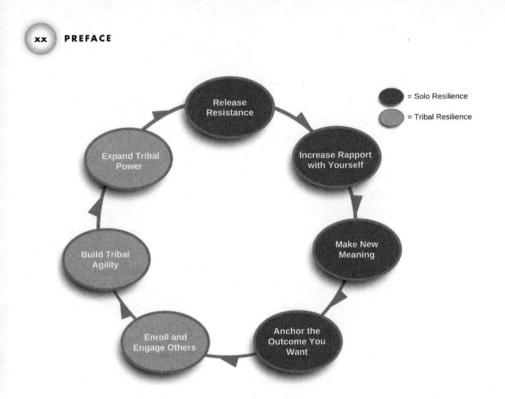

Figure P.1 The Resilience Cycle

And because just understanding the process isn't enough, to help you and your team move through each stage in the Resilience Cycle, you'll also receive a set of super powerful and effective tools that are easy to learn and use. Together, the process and tools make up your change playbook. Your playbook will help you implement changes in your organization, whether those changes are simple or complex, local or global, or narrow or broad.

EMOTIONAL AGILITY + TOOLS = POWER

In Part I, "What Happens Inside When Change Happens Outside," you'll learn some foundational principles of how we experience the world—how we decide whether what is happening is "good" or "bad," how stimulus from outside events causes us to assign meaning to our experience, and how your emotions even affect your cells.

Essentially, a business is made of people: employees, key stakeholders, and its owners. Adjusting the way people in a business behave and perform adjusts the way the business behaves and performs in the market. There-fore, if we want to change our business performance in change scenarios, we must first understand how *people* perform in change scenarios so that we will know what needs to be adjusted (if necessary) to align with the business's performance objectives.

Based on this foundation, in Part II, "The *Power Your Tribe* Playbook," you'll build emotional agility in yourself and those you lead in the change situations you face right now. You'll learn the tools and the processes to release resistance, be fully present, make new meaning, anchor the outcome you want, and enroll and engage others in achieving that outcome—all the while building a resilient tribe that has predictable revenue, passionate teams, and profitable growth. You'll also learn how to raise the bar and help your team redefine their personal best.

Finally, in Part III, "The *Power Your Tribe* Playbook Case Studies," we will walk you through some client case studies that show you how to apply a specific mix of tools in a variety of contexts, such as leadership abusing power, competitive crushes, merger and acquisition stresses, and family business and board dysfunction.

At the end of the book you'll find the appendix, which includes a diagnostic chart (Table A.1) that you can use in any scenario that summarizes all the tools you now have in your toolbox so you will know when to use them and how.

This book is designed in a problem-promise-result format, so it's easy to see how our tools will help you accomplish your goals.

Change is the new constant. Use it to power your tribe.

PART **I**

WHAT HAPPENS INSIDE WHEN CHANGE HAPPENS OUTSIDE

How Human Beings Experience the World

We decide whether an experience is "good" or "bad," and the meaning we assign to our experience creates and reinforces our identity, beliefs, capabilities, and behavior.

"I need your help, Christine," said the chief revenue officer. "Our sales and marketing people are overwhelmed by constantly changing legislation, the new markets we're trying to penetrate are not opening up, we're missing revenue projections, and the board is increasing the pressure. Everyone is discouraged, and they know they need to shift their attitude, but they can't seem to do it. Healthcare is a tough enough business without all this internal turmoil!"

Have you ever been in this situation? External and internal factors are pressuring you, and there's no sign of relief. You've got to get everyone on board pronto, but all your efforts haven't worked. In the midst of it all, you're doing your best to have a "better attitude" about the whole scenario. In this organization's case, although the initial instinct was to throw more bodies, tools, or money at the problem, it was *not* what they needed. And it wasn't as simple as just telling themselves to feel better.

For organizations in similar circumstances, the real issue has nothing to do with what happened or what needs to be done. It's what it *means* that matters. The meaning determines how it feels. And if shifting their attitude doesn't feel good, they won't do it. They will stay stuck.

In a "perfect storm" scenario like this, we need to have tools to shift our state, which we'll cover in Part II. But before we can use the tools, we must understand how we experience and create our experiences in the world. We must start with our emotions.

Consider this for a moment: if I delivered a big chunk of marble to your doorstep, how would you feel? If you viewed it as an obstruction, you'd probably feel annoyed. But if you were a sculptor, you might celebrate—you'd have some new material to work with!

In this chapter, you'll learn about what I call the *Critter State* and the *Smart State*, and you'll see how shifting to the Smart State can help you and your teams view any situation the way a sculptor would. From the Smart State, teams can see new openings, new solutions, and new approaches. They can also reframe existing perceived problems and challenges as opportunities to work with rather than seeing them as obstructions working *against* them. Everything has its uses, even challenges and perceived limitations.

As you deepen your understanding of what it means to be human and explore how you experience and generate experience in the world, you'll become more able to honor and respect both your experiences and the experiences of others and to do so with less judgment. Because you'll come to fully understand that everyone is truly doing the best they can with the tools they currently have. And that experience *can* be adjusted to be made better.

As my mentor Carl Buchheit says, human beings will always reach for the best feeling available on their menu. The sales and marketing teams didn't lack power. They lacked choices on their menu. In other words, to feel more powerful, we don't need to turn off our emotions or ignore them. We just need to add better feelings to our menu. It's all about choices.

You'll also come to see that you're not alone—we're all in this together. And it's time for us all to have more tools. It's time for us to have more choices. It's time for us to feel more powerful—not in having power over others but in having power over our own experience and emotional state.

Here are some signs that there are opportunities for you to deepen the connection, choice, and appreciation of your experience. This chapter will help if you are experiencing the following:

- Internal conflict, in which part of you wants to do or be something yet doesn't, or part of you doesn't want to do or be something yet does

- Resistance to an internal or external experience, behavior, belief, person, idea, or situation

- Being stuck in a repetitive pattern that you no longer want

- Reacting from fear and negative meaning making rather than responding from choice and positive meaning making

- Desiring something better, but you are somehow not able to get it

To quote the late great Wayne Dyer, "Change the way you look at things, and the things you look at change."[1] This is the good news. Not only can you learn emotional regulation and optimize the performance of your prefrontal cortex, you can also define the experience you want and create it. That's how powerful you are.

Our journey together in this chapter will help you understand the following:

1. How we decide whether what is happening to us is good or bad

2. How stimulus from outside events causes us to assign meaning to our experience

3. How this meaning reinforces our beliefs and identity

4. How our behaviors then match and further reinforce them

THE LOGICAL LEVELS OF CHANGE

According to anthropologist Gregory Bateson, humans experience change at certain levels.[2] At STI, we see these levels as concentric circles where change can occur outside in, inside out, or both simultaneously. Figure 1.1 shows how the circles work.

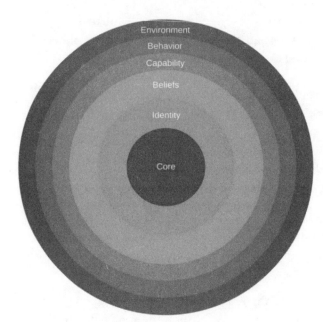

Environment:
Your physical, emotional, mental space.

Behavior:
What you do, your actions. The values that people or organizations hold contribute to defining their behavior.

Capability:
Your skills, tools, abilities.

Beliefs:
The decisions (meaning) you make about things outside of you: the organization, the world, a situation ("They are . . .," "It is . . . ").

Identity:
The decisions (meaning) you make about yourself ("I am . . .").

Core:
What is most sacred in your life or at the organization: your purpose or its purpose.

Figure 1.1 Logical Levels of Change

Source: Figure adapted and modified from initial work by
Gregory Bateson and Robert Dilts.

When we are challenged by external change, many Logical Levels of Change are affected. I'll give you an example. Let's say leadership has decided to relocate a team, overnight, to a new business market that speaks a foreign language. If that team were told they had to continue to grow the business *and* sustain its core mission, everyone would initially panic. It would be a big shock to the system.

This external change of moving to a new business market demands that the team do the following:

- *Adapt to a new environment* or adjust it to suit their needs. For example, they would be breathing in new air, eating new food perhaps, and living in new quarters. They might have to adjust to working in a new office environment (such as high-rise accommodations) or adjust to living farther away from the office than they used to.

- *Behave differently.* They might have to wake up at a different time and use different modes of transportation to get to work.

- *Develop new capabilities.* They may need to learn a new language or learn how to work with a translator in order to effectively communicate with the new customers and the new community.

- *Expand their beliefs* to include their colleagues and customers in this new world as collaborative, receptive, and welcoming.

- *Expand their identity* to include that they could work in this environment successfully.

All of these would support their *core* because they wouldn't be making the change if it didn't honor their mission or purpose (or the change would be short-lived!).

As we navigate these levels of change, it's essential that we also manage our mind. So let's consider what's happening in our brain as these changes are occurring.

MANAGING YOUR MIND: THE CRITTER STATE AND THE SMART STATE

Your brain has three essential parts: the reptilian brain, the mammalian brain, and the prefrontal cortex. We find the "triune brain" system proposed by neuroscientist Paul D. MacLean (1913 to 2007) to be a simple and effective model for the very complex human brain.[3] MacLean found from his work that the human brain is really three brains in one (hence "triune brain"). He also coined the term *limbic system*:

1. **The reptilian brain, or protoreptilian brain (includes the brain stem, midbrain, and basal ganglia):** The first part is located in the brain stem, and it sits at the base of the skull. It's the oldest and most primitive part of the brain, and it governs basic life-support systems such as breathing, feeding, sexuality, dominance, aggression, temperature regulation, and balance. It acts out of instinct, and it is primarily a stimulus-response machine with survival as its goal. It does not understand quality of life. It understands only dead and not dead. The reptilian brain is also where sensory information (sight, sound, touch, smell, and taste) enters our brain.

2. **The mammalian brain, or paleo-mammalian brain (includes the amygdala, hippocampus, hypothalamus, and other structures in**

the limbic system): The second part governs emotion, motivational systems, learning, short-term memory, and the body's response to danger (that is, how we respond to external stimuli, instincts, and past experiences). The key player here is the *limbic system*—that is, the emotional center of the brain that determines our fight/flight/freeze/faint response. The mammalian brain's primary focus is also survival, though it is additionally the seat of the more sophisticated emotions of separation distress, social emotions, maternal nurturance, anger, frustration, happiness, and love.

3. **The neocortex, or neo-mammalian brain:** This part of the brain is the newest and most evolved part of the brain. The prefrontal cortex within the neocortex enables us to plan, innovate, solve complex problems, think abstract thoughts, and have visionary ideas. It allows us to measure the quality of our experience, compare it to an abstract ideal, and yearn for change. It also allows us to have a number of advanced behaviors, including social connection, toolmaking, language, envisioning possible futures, and higher-level consciousness. It helps us to determine the *meaning* of the sensory information we've taken in via the reptilian brain.

If we combine the limbic system in the mammalian brain with the survival mechanism in the reptilian brain, we have the powerful combo pack we'll call the *critter brain*, as my mentor Carl Buchheit of NLP Marin terms it.[4] Once our critter brain has equated a particular phenomenon with safety or survival, it will do so as long as we are not dead because, again, it doesn't care about quality of life—it cares only about survival.

For example, if you watch a herd of antelope being chased by a cheetah, you'll see that their strategies for escape aren't incredibly elaborate. They all react the same: it's everyone for themselves; run, run, run! And no matter how much they know they are at the top of a cheetah's "to eat" list, they don't update their approach to avoiding death the next time a cheetah is on the hunt.

For the purpose of simplicity, we'll distill this to two states. The first is the *Critter State*, in which we don't have access to all parts of our brain and thus are reactive, in fight/flight/freeze/faint mode—that is, we are running safety programs (Figure 1.2). The second is the *Smart State*, in which we have easy access to all of our resources and can respond from choice (Figure 1.3).

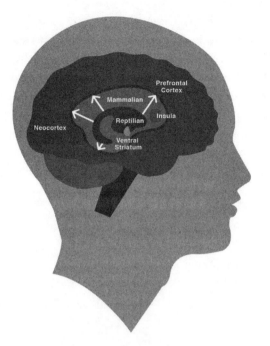

Figure 1.2 The Critter State

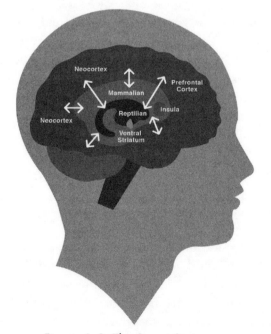

Figure 1.3 The Smart State

Just like the antelope, when a business is facing a threat, its people often go into Critter State. Communication stops, and teamwork goes down the drain. People may get aggressive or territorial, or they may behave in an "Everyone has to fend for themselves" manner. They retreat to what is familiar rather than pause to assess the situation and make decisions from a more resourceful state.

What kinds of threats put us in Critter State? Well, change itself, for one. Our brains just don't like change very much. It's scary to the most primal parts that are hardwired to ensure that we are safe and we survive, which means the critter brain will want to keep things basically the same whenever possible because "same" equals "safe."

Unfortunately, our behaviors in Critter State tend to create an environment where there is no or very low trust (often due to poor communication, constantly changing directives, high uncertainty, and/or excessive workloads), which exacerbates our Critter State. So we aren't creative, we aren't looking to innovate, and we aren't seeking opportunity. We're all about survival.

In contrast, when we're in the Smart State, all three parts of our brain are firing on all cylinders. We have flexibility, power, choice, balance. If we receive an angry e-mail from someone, we say, "Sounds like he's having a hard day," instead of reacting with fight/flight/freeze/faint.

Change and growth depend on making sure the Smart State—not the Critter State—is driving management decisions and behavior. There's already enough fear when things are changing, so it's essential to continuously help people see that they are safe, they belong, and they matter, so they can shift into the Smart State.

More on this soon, but first let's look at how we create the experiences that lead to either the Critter State or the Smart State—and how it affects the workplace.

HOW YOU CREATE EXPERIENCES

Every moment we are bombarded with sensory information. Visual, auditory, kinesthetic, olfactory, and gustatory information is constantly coming our way via our five senses. The way we interpret this sensory input contributes to the way we structure our experience of the world. The senses that most dominate our behavior are visual, auditory, and kinesthetic, so we'll focus on those three.

What we call "thinking" is actually a series of pictures, sounds, and feelings that go by at light speed in our brains. The process by which this happens is illustrated and summarized in Figure 1.4.

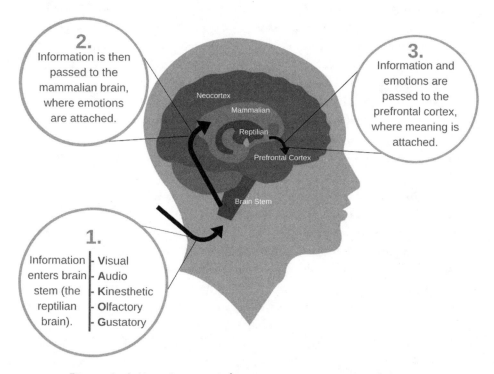

2.
Information is then passed to the mammalian brain, where emotions are attached.

3.
Information and emotions are passed to the prefrontal cortex, where meaning is attached.

Neocortex
Mammalian
Reptilian
Prefrontal Cortex
Brain Stem

1.
Information enters brain stem (the reptilian brain).
- Visual
- Audio
- Kinesthetic
- Olfactory
- Gustatory

Figure 1.4 How Sensory Information Is Processed in the Brain

As we interact with the world around us, we internally store images, sounds, feelings, smells, and tastes that craft our experience.

Think of your favorite place in your home. Chances are good that you just called up a picture. We'll call these *visuals*, or Vs in neuro-shorthand. Sometimes our brain distorts stored pictures (Vs) to give them different meanings. Maybe we don't want the intensity of a full-color picture so we store it in black and white, or maybe our brain wants to prevent us from repeating a dangerous experience so we store it in overpowering color.

Additionally, when we have or recall an experience, our brain hears sounds, which can be tones or words either outside ourself (existing in the environment) or inside ourself (talking to ourself, hearing an old sound track). Think of the last time you made a mistake and internally said, "I can't believe I did that! Sheesh!" That's an internal sound track. Think of the sound of a phone ringing. That's an external sound track. We'll call these sounds *auditory* input, or As in neuro-shorthand.

Our visual and auditory experiences lead to feelings, or *kinesthetic responses*, or Ks in neuro-shorthand. Maybe your shoulders are tight or you feel a knot in your stomach. These physiological feelings are now translated into emotions you can name, such as fear, excitement, joy, or anger.

From these Vs, As, and their generated Ks, our prefrontal cortex makes meaning about the world, other people, situations, and ourselves. The meaning we make about these experiences formulates our beliefs.

Before we discuss beliefs, we must understand that the brain is a "meaning-making machine" that deletes, distorts, and generalizes information. Every second, overwhelming amounts of information come our way, and we filter that information to make sense of it by *deleting* a lot of what we deem not relevant or useful so that only some of it gets through. Otherwise we would experience information overload!

The brain also *distorts* information. For example, how often do you hear someone respond to the question "How are you?" with "Nothing is wrong with me!" The question was distorted to be the assertion "Something is wrong with you." However, distortion also has its uses. It is what allows us to be creative. For example, a musician can listen to a song and create a new version of it as his or her unique expression.

Beliefs are *generalizations* about experiences, based on the meaning our prefrontal cortex has generated. For example, the brain generalizes that a chair is a chair, and objects that resemble a chair-like structure are appropriate for sitting. This is useful. That way, we don't have to figure out whether we can sit on a particular object every time we walk into an office.

Another example is when we see someone point a finger at another and assume that the person doing the pointing is rude. "Everyone who points his or her finger like that is a rude person!" is a generalization and a belief.

Our beliefs about the world, others, situations, and ourselves drive our *behavior*. Beliefs about ourselves lie at a deeper level and are called *identity*. So in a stressful situation, when a person believes, "I can do this, and our team will get through this," these beliefs reinforce his or her identity and his or her team's identity as being solid and capable. As a result, the person with the "solid and capable" identity has the behavior of handling things and moving forward, while others may be panicking. Their behavior matches their identity.

So here's how Vs, As, and Ks work together to create a new experience based on what you've already stored. Let's say you walk into a conference room you've never been in before to deliver a high-stakes presentation, and the phone on the table rings. Your brain probably already has "conference room pictures" stored, so you instantly associate that ring tone with a stored picture of another conference room from a different time and place, one in which you totally rocked a presentation and your boss called you afterward to congratulate you on a job well done. That external trigger (hearing the telephone in the conference room) ignited a whole series of stored internal Vs and As that now lead to a whopping great positive K and the belief "My boss appreciates me!" You've never been in this room before, and you were a little nervous, but all you know now is that you feel great and you really like that phone.

The sound of the telephone in that setting is an *anchor* that invokes the experience of confidence and creates positive meaning for you. Here's how it worked in your brain:

$$V \text{ (image of phone in conference room)} + A \text{ (ring tone)} = K \text{ (confidence)}$$

This sequence then leads to this:

$$\text{Belief ("My boss appreciates me!")} \rightarrow \text{identity ("I am valued")} \rightarrow \text{capability (confident and competent in business scenarios)}$$

And you know what happens next: your behavior will match your beliefs, identity, and capability—in other words, the meaning you associate with these sensory experiences.

By the way, what makes this really interesting is that we can anchor those reference experiences to something new (a space, a sound, or a touch) to create the meaning we would like to create. That is to say, we can adjust the equation variables of V, A, and K to create a new set of beliefs. The tool that helps us achieve this is called *Anchoring*, and we'll cover it in detail in Chapter 6.

WHY YOU DO WHAT YOU DO

Every day, all day, we are having experiences, creating meaning and forming new or reinforcing old beliefs, and forging a new identity or reinforcing our current one.

Let's create an experience right now. Close your eyes and recall a positive memory, a time when you had a positive experience. Do this now, and then answer the following questions about your positive memory when the experience is super clear:

- What did you see?

- What did you hear outside or inside yourself (maybe you heard yourself saying, "This is awesome!")?

- What did you feel?

- What did you decide (believe) about the situation and others and the world?

- What did you decide about yourself (your identity)?

For example, perhaps you recalled a recent team meeting:

- In it, you *saw* (Vs) everyone gathered around the table, excited, alert, ready to roll.

- You *heard* (As) people offering suggestions, brainstorming, making commitments. Inside you heard yourself say, "This is great—I love meetings like this. We're accomplishing things. We're all in sync."

- You *felt* (Ks) powerful, optimistic, positive.

- You *believed* these were the right people in the right roles.

- Your *identity* that you are successful, you are a good leader, and you are adding value was reinforced.

The problem arises when we believe in a way that *doesn't* create the best possible outcome. For the next week, please start to notice what associations you have with places and people. What feelings (Ks) do you get from certain sounds (As) and certain visuals (Vs)? What meaning do you make from the experience of the resulting positive or negative feeling (K+ or K−), and what does that cause you to do?

Let's reflect on the situation I shared at the start of the chapter, in which the sales and marketing teams felt powerless due to constantly changing legislation, competitive markets, decreasing revenue, and the board's increasing the pressure. It makes you wonder: What beliefs were governing their experience? What meaning did they make from the Vs, As, and Ks that caused them to feel powerless to make a change?

In Part II, you're going to learn how to deactivate your own and your team members' fear triggers and instead assign appropriate meaning so that you can help shift people from the Critter State to the Smart State. You're going to learn exactly what to do to create a team that acts as a team, helping each other outperform the competition—an emotionally agile team that is resilient in the face of constant change.

Now that you understand how you create experiences, there's just one more foundational concept to cover before we can leap into action: the three things all humans crave. We'll cover those in the next chapter.

SUMMARY

1. Human beings have three parts to their brain: the reptilian, the mammalian, and the neo cortex. We generally occupy one of two states, depending on which parts of our brain are "lit up": the Critter State (fight/flight/freeze/faint) or the Smart State (connection, ease, choice).

2. We can learn to move from the Critter State to the Smart State so that we can be more resourceful in response to a turbulent internal or external environment. To do so, we must adjust the way the different parts of our brain process information.

3. Information from the external environment is stored as *visual, auditory, kinesthetic, olfactory,* and *gustatory* (VAKOG) data in our brains. Our prefrontal cortex assigns meaning to the information, primarily by generating beliefs.

4. If the feeling assigned to the information (person, place, thing, or activity) is bad, then the meaning we make of that information will be, "It is bad." Similarly, if the feeling assigned to the information feels good, then the meaning we make of the information will be, "It is good."

5. Human beings will reach only for the best available feeling on their menu. If we want to change behavior, we must add *new* and *better* feelings to the menu, *not* remove bad ones.

TWITTER TAKEAWAYS

- We must understand how we create our experiences in the world, and that starts with understanding our emotions.

- Feeling more powerful is not about turning off our emotions or ignoring them. It's about making choices. It's about making better emotions available.

- It's time for us to feel more powerful—not in having power over others but in having power over our own experience and emotional state.

- Change and growth depend on making sure that the Smart State—not the Critter State—is driving management decisions and behavior.

- If we want to change behavior, we must add new and better feelings to the menu, not remove bad ones.

RESOURCES

See this chapter's section on www.PowerYourTribe.com for the following:

- Chapter *Quick Summary* video
- Culture and sharing values examples
- *Create the Culture of Your Dreams* video
- *Leading from the Inside Out* kit
- *Your Awesome Brain and How It Works* video

The Three Things All Humans Crave

Resilient teams have three key ingredients: safety, belonging, and mattering.

We all want things to continuously get better, especially in times of change and uncertainty. That's what it means to be human. Now that you've learned how you create experiences, let's focus on how you make your current experience better.

YOU ARE HERE, BUT YOU WANT TO BE THERE

Let's map this out (Figure 2.1). We'll call where you currently are, your current experience of the world, the *Present State* (PS). And there are situations or experiences in your PS that you either don't like or want to improve. Maybe you've had a big layoff, or you need to fill a crucial role and recruiting is taking too long, or a new competitor is eroding what used to be a reliable revenue base. Maybe your business and organization are doing well with bottom-line growth and market penetration, but you want to explore ways to enter new markets to expand your impact and generate greater profits and you can't seem to find the time.

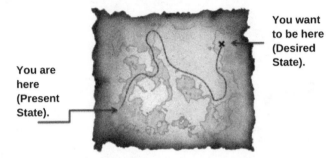

You want to be here (Desired State).

You are here (Present State).

Figure 2.1 Mapping Your Desired Destination

Your envisioned *Desired State* (DS) is that "better" place, the place where you will have achieved and/or received what you wanted back in your PS, the place where you can navigate change easily and powerfully.

For example, you may want to shift the way you're thinking about a big layoff, moving from the PS of seeing it as a painful experience to the DS of seeing it as an opportunity to reduce expenses and streamline staff to peak performers. You may want to move from the PS of a slow recruiting process to the DS of an optimal process that gets you more great candidates and allows you to onboard and cultivate new hires more quickly. Or you may want to move from the PS of an eroding revenue base to the DS of developing new product lines and key sales channels.

Now, think of the terrain on the map between our PS and DS as something that can change at any moment. And as the terrain changes, the path from the PS to the DS must change too. New trajectories and pathways must be formed. Emotional agility is what enables you to do that with certainty, precision, and swiftness.

No matter where you start, where you're going, or how you get there, you're going to need three things for your journey. They're the three key ingredients of emotional agility: *safety*, *belonging*, and *mattering*.

WHERE IT ALL BEGINS:
THE THREE THINGS HUMANS CRAVE

Maslow was right.[1] Before we can seek self-actualization, we must feel safety, belonging, and mattering (Figure 2.2). Without them, people cannot get in their Smart State (self-actualization)—they cannot perform, innovate, feel emotionally engaged, agree, or move forward.

**Figure 2.2 Abraham Maslow's Hierarchy of Needs
with a Few Modern Edits**

Source: Figure adapted and modified from the original work of Abraham Maslow.

After food, water, shelter, warmth, and good Wi-Fi service, safety, belonging, and mattering are the three things human beings crave. All three are great Ks (feelings), and they drive and dominate human behavior.

These three key emotional experiences govern how emotionally agile—or fragile—human beings are. When they aren't working properly, human beings will feel like spun glass, ready to break at any moment. When they are working properly, human beings gain greater emotional agility—they become like water, having the capacity to flow around many forms of resistance.

First, the greater the feeling of *safety*, both emotional and physical, the more we feel able to take risks because safety reduces the experience of risk.

Safety means creating an environment where there is freedom from fear, where we can take risks and stretch and grow. Is it safe to take risks at your organization?

What's true for you and your team is true for your clients. If they're stuck in fear, they won't reach for your business offering. So the first step in any sales or marketing scenario is to generate safety. Generating safety for customers can take the form of guarantees of any type, service agreements, and/or social proof about how you came through for other clients in similar situations. More about this later in the book.

Second, the greater the feeling of *belonging* with others, or the feeling that we're in this together, the more alignment we have as a team, a family, and a tribe.

Belonging means creating an environment where we all feel like a tight-knit tribe, we're all equal, and we're all rowing in the same direction to reach our goals. Think about gangs—where people will literally kill to stay in the tribe. That's how powerful the need to belong is.

In your business, creating a sense of belonging means creating a compelling mission, vision, and values so that your team knows *how* to belong: they belong by honoring the values as they live the mission and aspire to the vision. For your clients, you can build an online community; host physical events, conferences, or annual meetings; and share testimonials or news about how well a recent gathering went. These efforts also help your clients view you as partners rather than vendors. Belonging builds brand loyalty, improves customer retention, and increases penetration per client account.

And third, the greater the feeling that we personally *matter*, make a difference, and are contributing to the greater good, the greater the success of the organization, the relationship, the family, the team, the individual.

Mattering means each of us contributes individually in a unique way. We all make a difference. We're appreciated and publicly acknowledged. Does your organization's culture work this way?

Of course, mattering is just as important to your customers. To increase their experience of mattering, you can use customer satisfaction surveys, celebrate their successes, and provide loyalty and/or retention programs. These all help communicate that the customers matter, that they deserve attention, and that they affect the world. Mattering helps build brand awareness *and* brand loyalty.

None of us actually buy products or services. We buy emotional experiences of safety, belonging, and mattering. What emotional experience are you providing to your team? To your clients? To the marketplace? More on this in Chapter 7.

HOW SAFETY, BELONGING, AND MATTERING GET YOU TO YOUR DESIRED STATE

Let me give you a real-life example of how safety, belonging, and mattering help us get from our Present State to our Desired State.

Dave and Robert had built a thriving business. Revenues and profits had grown consistently as their digital marketing firm gained fame, won numerous awards, and grew a clientele that included the A list of consumer brands.

Together Dave and Robert had the "secret sauce." Dave was the flamboyant creative with remarkable vision—heck, he could make floor wax seem sexy. Clients loved Dave and felt invigorated in his presence. He made them want to do great things, expand projects, make the world a better place. Dave was a natural salesperson too.

Robert was the operations, finance, and process guy. He kept all the pieces in their complex projects moving forward, he tempered Dave's ideas when they would've eroded a project's profitability, and he kept the staff happy and the business running. Dave and Robert needed each other. And their clients needed them. Going solo wasn't really an option—and Robert knew it.

Then things changed. After Dave's divorce, he became a different person: he was unaccountable, he arrived late in the office and left early, he wasn't prepared for client presentations, and he blamed all mistakes on the junior staff. Meanwhile, Robert was working insanely long hours to cover Dave's constantly missed deadlines. Robert's family was asking when they'd get more time with him because he worked nights and weekends in the office. By the time Robert called us, he was ready to buy Dave out and go solo. He'd already called his attorney.

Dave now needed to *matter* (in his personal life and at work) more than ever before and was searching for where he could now *belong* (since he no longer belonged with his wife). Dave's way of mattering meant doing what he wanted, when he wanted, how he wanted—which didn't work well with the organization's agenda. He was also withdrawing and isolating himself from his work tribe, where he would have gotten tremendous support if only he could have shifted out of Critter State to benefit from it.

Robert needed to feel *safe* ("Would Dave really show up?") and *belong* ("If we're in this together, I need him to honor his promises to me"). When Robert felt unsafe, he would micromanage, become hypervigilant, and wait for the next disaster to strike. This wasn't very much fun for the team. The team also missed Dave's wackiness and spark. Robert began withholding information from Dave because he figured he couldn't count on him anyway. This led to more trouble.

Robert and Dave both found themselves operating from the Critter State. However, they wanted to make their relationship and business work again, and they were willing to invest in it. So we coached them both as individuals separately to work through their own challenges and as partners together to forge a new commitment to one another and the business. The result was clarity about each other's experience, what they needed most from each other, and what they needed most from the business.

Because Dave's experience of mattering meant doing what he wanted, when he wanted, and how he wanted, Dave needed and got more flexible working hours as he redesigned his life, a reduced workload for six months (which enabled his second-in-command to rise up), and the assurance that he would be called upon to deliver client presentation work only for key accounts. More mattering and belonging.

Dave's temporary plan worked well for Robert because what he needed most was to know what he could count on Dave for. Dave's second-in-command worked closely with Robert whenever he felt concerned or unsure about project status and milestones. This brought Robert more safety.

With safety, belonging, and mattering firmly in place, the partnership was reinvigorated, both partners became more compassionate with each other, the staff was relieved and able to refocus on work rather than the prior partner conflict, and Dave's second-in-command landed some huge new accounts. The business was once again thriving!

The greater the experience of safety, belonging, and mattering, the more resilient we are and the more we can adapt and pivot to meet change and growth—for ourselves and our customers. In every communication, in every conflict, we are subconsciously either reinforcing or asking for safety, belonging, or mattering (or a combination of the three). It's neurological, and it's primal—there is nothing you can do to override or change this subconscious programming, as much as you may try.

WHERE YOU CRAVE SAFETY, BELONGING, AND MATTERING

Safety, belonging, and mattering are prevalent in your life and your organization—let's see where with a quick quiz. For each behavior below, what is the person craving: safety, belonging, or mattering?

1. Fight/flight/freeze/faint craves _____.

2. Talking about "us versus them" craves _____.

3. Victim and/or complaining craves _____.

4. Perpetually seeking recognition craves _____.

5. Procrastination and/or perfectionism craves _____.

What are the answers? (1) Safety, (2) belonging, (3) mattering, (4) mattering, and (5) a combo of mattering and safety. Sure, 1 through 4 could crave all three, but it's helpful to look at what is most essential and then to provide that. It gets results faster.

So as a leader, and as a human, in any given situation, you must identify whether safety and/or belonging and/or mattering is most important to the people in your life and then do everything you can to satisfy those subconscious needs:

Safety + belonging + mattering = trust

This means leaders must behave in ways that make employees feel that they are safe, that they belong, and that they matter. Doing so will help shift them out of their fear-driven Critter State (where all decisions are based on what they perceive will help them survive) and into their Smart State (where they can innovate, collaborate, feel emotionally engaged, and move the organization forward).

Remember, this isn't just true of employees. It's true of clients, associates, spouses, friends, children. At our emotional core, we all want safety, belonging, and mattering. To influence anyone, we must influence emotionally. (We'll dive into the specifics in Chapter 7.)

WHAT CRITTER STATE CAUSES TO HAPPEN INSIDE YOU—AND OTHERS

You'll recall from Chapter 1 that Critter State occurs based on how we interpret the sensory input we receive. Vs, As, and Ks enter the reptilian brain and then move into the mammalian brain, where emotions are determined based on Ks (the feeling of "tightness" in your stomach is translated to the emotion of stress), which then leads to meaning making in the prefrontal cortex—specifically about whether safety, belonging, and/or mattering are needed or are already in place (in that case, yay!). If, as a result of all this, we are in Critter State, a series of actions occurs in our body to perpetuate Critter State—that is, if we don't learn some new tools.

As we also mentioned in Chapter 1, when people go into their Critter State as a result of change alone, they often feel disengaged, disconnected, and stressed, experiencing chaos, distrust, and even aggression. On top of that, during times of change, we often see teams struggle with excessive workload because resources are scarce. So what happens? Multitasking, as we scramble to get on top of everything we need to do. In the United States, multitasking is often expected and even rewarded, but science shows us that it's just another way to make Critter State worse.

According to the work of Susan Greenfield at Oxford, heavy multitasking reduces density in the part of the brain called the *anterior cingulate cortex* (ACC).[2] The ACC is involved in a number of functions, but let's focus on the cognitive ones crucial to change scenarios, which include reward anticipation, decision-making, empathy, impulse control, and emotion. When we have less gray matter density in the ACC, over time we see a reduced ability to make sound decisions, modulate our emotions, empathize, and connect with others.

All of this, of course, creates even more stress in all areas of our lives—in our organization's culture, our relationships, and ourselves.

Stress doesn't affect just our cognitive functions. It affects our bodies too. Stress causes the body to release *cortisol*, which triggers the release of *cytokines*—proteins key in cell signaling. Cytokines affect the behavior of many cells affecting cognitive and immune function (see Figure 2.3), and excessive cytokines can lead to the following:

- Being easily emotionally triggered
- Immune system damage

- Learning challenges

- Difficulty organizing

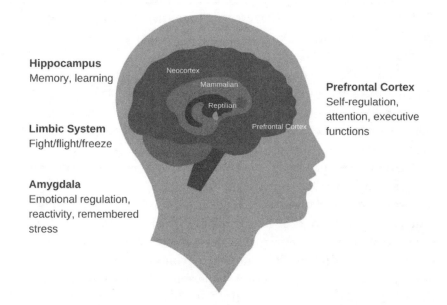

Figure 2.3 The Effects of Cytokines on the Brain

What can we do? As leaders, we need to give ourselves and our tribe the three things we all crave:

- **Safety:** "I can take risks and not be ostracized or penalized."

- **Belonging:** "These are my people, my tribe. They understand me, and I fit in here."

- **Mattering:** "I am seen, acknowledged for my gifts, and appreciated."

That's it. Safety, belonging, and mattering are the three things we need to declare complete devotion to another person, a cause, or an organization. They're the three things we need to hang in there when the going gets tough. They're the three things we need to be in our Smart State and to navigate change easily and powerfully.

So why do we so often fail to inspire these emotional experiences in those in need? Because we are in Critter State too.

HOW YOUR BRAIN
BLOCKS PERFORMANCE

While we're craving the experience of safety, belonging, and mattering, and while we're wanting *out* of our Present State and *in* to our Desired State, we have a bit of a dilemma: even when we know what we *should* do, our brain is still working against itself.

Our default behaviors become "baked in" at an early age, and generally most of them help us survive. If a behavior helps us survive—or to say it more accurately, if our brain has "coded" the behavior as "something that helps us survive"—we will keep doing it because we are wired to stay "not dead," thanks to our reptilian brain.

Here's where it gets tricky: the more a neural pathway is used, the more of a default behavior it becomes. As neurobiologist Carla Shatz says, "Cells that fire together wire together."[3] This is why some of our most frequent reactions and/or behaviors operate at broadband speed, when they initially were at dial-up speed. Neuropsychologist and father of neural networks Donald O. Hebb explained this through his concept of Hebbian potentiation.[4] The cortex develops "grooves of meaning," like a long-playing (LP) record (for those of you familiar with vinyl LPs), so it is conditioned to ask for the same data (Vs, As, and Ks) over and over. This is why change can be hard: we have to deliberately create new pathways to potentiate new grooves of meaning. This is what we do in neuroscience-based executive coaching, and it's why this book's change playbook gives you a toolbox with the instruction manual.

EMOTIONAL AGILITY + TOOLS = POWER

Now that we understand where change occurs (the Logical Levels of Change), how humans make meaning, and what humans crave emotionally, and we have a basic understanding of the physiology causing all of this, it's time to learn the tools and process to create the experience we want for ourselves and others—and to use change as fuel to power ourselves and our tribe.

In Part II, "The *Power Your Tribe* Playbook," you'll learn how to choose the meaning you make; bring safety, belonging, and mattering to yourself and others; get clear on the outcomes you want and anchor them in your physiology; and continually increase emotional agility in your tribe so that you can pursue those outcomes together.

SUMMARY

1. Establishing safety, belonging, and mattering is a prerequisite for self-actualization, the Smart State, and emotional agility. Without those three essentials, a person or team cannot perform, innovate, feel emotionally engaged, agree, or move forward.

2. Whenever you face a challenge, consider how you can bring more safety, belonging, and mattering to the situation and the people involved.

3. Safety, belonging, and mattering are already prevalent in your life and organization. The question is not whether they are there. It is whether they are increasing or decreasing and whether they are stable or highly variable.

4. Change, adversity, or turbulence places excessive stress on a business's people. Excessive stress adversely affects all key cognitive systems, including memory, learning, self-regulation, attention, executive functions, and emotional regulation.

5. Our default behaviors become "baked in" at an early age, and generally most of them help us survive. If our brain has "coded" a behavior as "survival related," it will keep running that behavior until we learn how to change it.

TWITTER TAKEAWAYS

- Before we can seek self-actualization—the Smart State—we must feel safety, belonging, and mattering.

- Safety, belonging, and mattering are essential to your brain and your ability to perform at work, at home, and in life.

- None of us actually buy products or services. We buy emotional experiences of safety, belonging, or mattering.

- Safety + belonging + mattering = trust.

- With safety, belonging, and mattering, we can navigate change because we aren't alone. We're in it together with our tribe.

RESOURCES

See this chapter's section on www.PowerYourTribe.com for the following:

- Chapter *Quick Summary* video

- *The Brain-Based Secrets of Optimal Teams* video

- Behavioral Stances: How to Be Less Predictable as a Leader

THE *POWER YOUR TRIBE* PLAYBOOK: LEARN TO *LOVE* CHANGE

CHAPTER 3

Release Resistance

Resistance stabilizes the Present State, which is where the problem is. Learn how to release resistance so you can be more agile and have more choice.

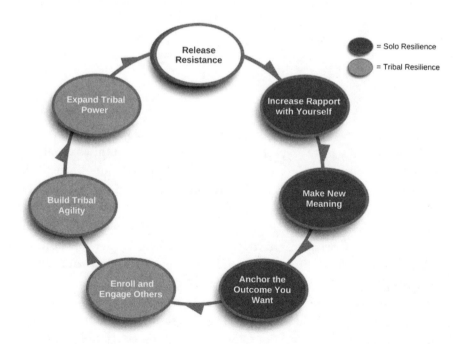

Figure 3.1 The Resilience Cycle: Release Resistance

PROBLEM

The marketing team of a major food organization (mentioned in the preface) was stressed out. They'd suffered huge losses in some key brands due to fake news on social media saying their products were unsafe. To make the challenge even greater, times were changing and consumers wanted more healthful food with fewer ingredients. They had trusted our client in the past but now were reluctant to.

An entirely new marketing approach was required to turn around the negative perception and highlight the new recipes and ingredients in the updated products. Headquarters wanted this new approach now, with campaigns launching within 60 days, and high revenue targets were established and expected to be met in the following 90 days.

The team was saying this was impossible. They couldn't pivot this fast. They were resisting the entire experience, so they fell into victim thinking and had countless meetings, telling HQ that it simply wasn't possible and they were being set up for failure. People were ready to quit. They knew change was needed, but they were stuck in overwhelm, anger, and anxiety. Leadership called a five-day all-hands meeting to forge new strategies and lay out their 60-day plan.

PROMISE

Yes, there was a lot to accomplish in the next five days: finalizing and then pitching the new marketing initiative to headquarters, reorganizing and reassigning many direct reports to new teams, and an omni-channel approach to rebuild trust and enroll external brand ambassadors. To get it all done, we needed to shift the emotional state first of the 15 regional leaders and then that of their teams.

Starting with the regional leaders, we used the *Emotion Wheel* (which we'll cover in this chapter) to help individuals identify the emotions in their Present State (which were in the sad, mad, and scared categories). To help shift their emotional state toward empowerment, we taught them how to use the *Maneuvers of Consciousness* tool in a guided buddy process so that each buddy could watch the other one shift. Throughout, the leaders checked in with our Emotion Wheel so that they could track their emotional agility. Fifteen minutes later, the first half of the group had shifted from the sad, mad, and scared sections to one or more of the emotions in the powerful, joyful, and peaceful categories. Fifteen more minutes and the other half had shifted.

Later we used the same tools to help their teams shift, which included the leaders' direct reports and some key stakeholders. Now we could get to work.

RESULT

As a result, the team was now able to be present, and they were telling themselves new, more powerful narratives. The environment in the room had completely transformed from constricting to expanding. People were standing up and writing down on flip charts how they'd achieve goals. The buzz and energy of possibility and enthusiasm were palpable. Some of the strongest naysayers volunteered to be spokespeople when the plan was presented to the executive team the next day.

We worked long hours in deep creativity, mapping out the final details and graphics for the executive presentation. The next morning the core team took the stage. The presentation was open and honest. They showed the upsides and downsides, and they forged a deep bond with the executive team. Finally, everyone was in this together.

Fast-forward just 90 days after the launch: revenue was starting to climb, online consumer evangelists were praising our client for valuing the voice of the consumer, and everything was coming together beautifully.

THE EMOTION WHEEL:
KNOW YOUR STARTING POINT

You may be familiar with the Chinese finger trap. It's a toy that traps the victim's fingers (often the index fingers) in both ends of a small cylinder woven from bamboo. The initial reaction of the victim is to pull his or her fingers outward, but this only tightens the trap.

Resisting our experience has the same effect. We resist things or situations or people we perceive as hurtful, painful, or threatening to our safety, belonging, or mattering. As you learned in Chapter 2, without these three key emotional experiences, we can't shift to our Smart State, and we can't navigate our constantly changing landscape to reach self-actualization. Also, as you learned in Chapter 1, we are wired to resist what we believe will create a worse K, or worse feeling, for us.

Resistance isn't necessarily bad. It's often simply the first step of navigating change. The goal is to move forward rather than get stuck resisting. Resistance shows that someone is engaged to a degree, which is much better than being disengaged, after all! Don't be surprised if resistance turns to mockery, as some people express their upset that way. As leaders, it's essential to move our team through this stage by asking what they are resisting, or what's annoying, dumb, or unreasonable about the particular change or initiative. Then we address what we can, with the agreement that they'll try the new initiative or plan. Ultimately they'll find some aspect of it to be useful; over time it will even become habitual, and then—voilà!— a new standard is established. Enjoy the afterglow . . . until the next change comes along.

The origin and etymology of *resist* (Late Middle English) is from the Latin *resistere*: *re-* (expressing opposition) + *sistere* (to stand). Aha! So *resistance* really means to stand in opposition. What are you taking a stand against?

Let's also take a look at *reject*, which is what we're doing when we are resisting our Present State. The origin and etymology of *reject* (Late Middle English) is from the Latin verb *rejacere*: *re-* (back) + *jacere* (to throw). Yikes. This is even worse than resisting. *Reject* means to throw back or throw against. This stance isn't just in opposition. It is opposing by *attack*.

The trouble with resistance is that it takes a tremendous amount of energy in the form of pushing back and rejecting. When we direct energy toward what we *don't* want, it actually helps draw it toward us. For example, the more you try to pull your fingers out of the Chinese finger trap, the tighter it becomes.

You've likely heard the expression "What we resist persists." Look at what you've resisted—did they stick around in your life longer than you would've liked? Resistance merely stabilizes your Present State and ensures that it continues, so the more you resist, the more you're work against creating your Desired State!

TRANSFORMING RESISTANCE: LETTING YOURSELF GET WHAT YOU WANT

Now that we're clear on what resistance is, let's consider the alternatives. First let me state that it's not acceptance. If your fingers are in the Chinese finger trap, accepting it isn't useful. It doesn't change anything. So what's our choice if we neither want to resist nor tolerate it?

It's *consent*. Consent doesn't mean something is OK. Consent simply means something just is, and resisting it isn't going to help. Better to put our energy where it can actually do some good.

The way to get out of the Chinese finger trap is to move your index fingers toward the middle of it, the narrow section. This enlarges the openings and frees the fingers. The solution is to work with it rather than against it.

> The origin and etymology of *consent* (Middle English) is from the Latin *con* (together) + *sentere* (feel). *Con* + *sentere* means to *feel* or *realize* with. *Consenting* doesn't mean agreeing, accepting, approving, condoning, surrendering, or any other synonyms you may be thinking of.
>
> It just means to *be present with*, essentially, without any other emotion or judgment attached to it. The opposite of consenting is resisting or rejecting.

Think of it as a spectrum. On one end is everything inside or outside of us that we are resisting in our Present State (PS). On the other end is everything we want in our Desired State (DS). The path that allows us to get from one end of the spectrum to the other is *consent*, where we cease to resist:

What we resist (PS) → consent → what we desire (DS)

> The origin and etymology of *desire* (Middle English) is from the Latin *desiderare*: *de* (from) + *sidere* (star, or heavenly body). Now we're talking! If *desire* means from a star, a heavenly body, this is getting more compelling.

To shift from Critter State to Smart State and give yourself more choice, we'll need to start where you are and transform your current resistance. To transform resistance, we use the power of consent—which, again, isn't saying something is OK but, rather, acknowledging reality and thereby destabilizing the Present State.

When we consent to our Present State, we can start to feel better. Then we can become more emotionally agile and have more choice to create our Desired State.

EMOTIONS HAVE ENERGY

We've all felt how draining fear-based emotions can be. Nothing saps our team's life force more than panic, overreaction, and upset that is unfounded. Thanks to David Hawkins, MD, PhD, we have proof that emotions have measurable energy and can either foster or negate actual cell life.

Dr. Hawkins's groundbreaking work, as explained in his book *Power vs. Force*, shows how a person's *log level* (that is, the measurable energy level in his or her magnetic field) increases as that person experiences more positive emotions.

Hawkins's most interesting finding was that cells actually died when the log level was below 200, where the emotions of scorn, hate, anxiety, shame, regret, despair, blame, and humiliation reside. This evidence provides us with further reason for us to regulate and manage our emotional state not just for our overall well-being (and that of those around us) but also for our physical health.

Tool: The Emotion Wheel

To consent to our emotions, we first need to know what they are. But only a select few of us can accurately identify our emotions as they occur. According to Travis Bradberry, author of *Emotional Intelligence 2.0*:

> Our research shows that only 36 percent of people can do this, which is problematic because unlabeled emotions often go misunderstood, which leads to irrational choices and counterproductive actions.[1]

Wow. Only 36 percent of people really know how they feel at any given time. The remaining 64 percent do not. We see it in our training sessions and executive coaching sessions all the time. This is why the Emotion Wheel is so helpful (Figure 3.2).

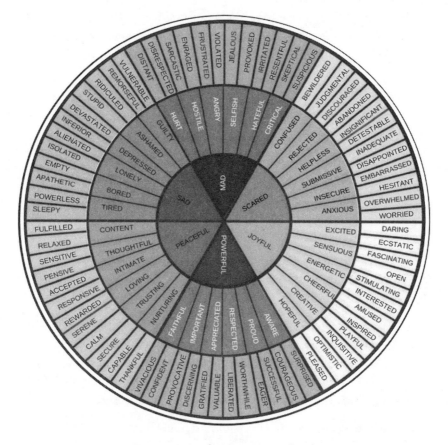

Figure 3.2 The Emotion Wheel

You can use the Emotion Wheel from the inside out to identify your primary emotions first and then move outward. Or you can move from the outside in if your specific emotion seems clear and you want to identify the primary emotion beneath it. Or you can simply pop around as you explore and identify how you feel.

Generally, we've found that people experiencing intense emotion will first identify with the main emotions in the inner "pie" slices, whereas those experiencing less intensity will often identify emotions on the very outer rim. Either way, when we can name how we feel, we become more present to our current situation. And we must be present before we can shift it. There are, of course, many emotions not on the wheel. Use this tool as a way to "prime the pump" so that you can then identify the emotion you are currently experiencing.

Here's a quick exercise to help you experience the energy of both resistance and consent, using the Emotion Wheel. Let's assume you're learning something new and you're a little bit confused. You now have a choice:

Confusion $\rightarrow$ *resistance and/or rejection* $\rightarrow$ frustration $\rightarrow$ anger $\rightarrow$ dismissal $\rightarrow$ reject learning

or:

Confusion $\rightarrow$ *consent* $\rightarrow$ curiosity $\rightarrow$ inquiry $\rightarrow$ open-mindedness and/or new perspective $\rightarrow$ embrace learning

Which path do you default to?

Which path would you *like* to default to?

To flex your ability to resist and then to consent, try the following exercise. Make sure to have the Emotion Wheel handy:

- Walk around and identify 10 things in your life or in the world you don't want or like. Make sure they are things you can see in your physical space (tacky wallpaper in your kitchen, a few extra pounds on your tummy). To each one, say out loud, "I do not consent to you." (By this you mean, it's *not* OK that they are there.)

- See how saying that feels in your body. Feel free to use the Emotion Wheel.

- Break this emotional state by shaking your body out or jumping up and down for a few seconds.

- Look at the 10 things again. They still exist even though you didn't consent to them! Hmmm. Now say to each of the 10 things, "I consent to you." (Heck, they are there anyway, so there's not much point in resisting the fact. Consent isn't approval. It's just acknowledgment.)

- See how that feels in your body, using the Emotion Wheel as needed.

- Reflect on the feelings associated with not consenting and/or resistance to what is versus consenting to and/or acknowledging what is.

It's OK if things aren't OK with you. Notice what it's like to let them not be OK *and* acknowledge that they are there without energetically resisting them.

Excellent. This exercise was actually a warm-up to using one of my favorite tools to shift from resistance to consent all the way to full appreciation: Maneuvers of Consciousness.

MANEUVERS OF CONSCIOUSNESS: FROM RESISTANCE TO CONSENT TO APPRECIATION

Remember, whatever we focus on, we fuel. When we resist an emotion, we make it stronger. But if we consent, we shift our relationship to the experience and loosen up our emotional experience. Once that is achieved, we are free to move to a different part of the Emotion Wheel. We have added more options to our menu of emotional choices.

We can maneuver, or change, our *consciousness* (that is, our current conscious emotional experience) quite easily. Human beings are inherently resilient; it's just that some of us haven't realized it yet. You will notice how your emotions regarding a given experience can shift from painful and "low log level" per Hawkins's research to higher log level and more empowering. All in a mere 15 minutes.

Tool: Maneuvers of Consciousness

First, think of something you are resisting. This time, pick something meaty, like a painful belief; a belittling, angry, or unpleasant person; or a situation you really don't want in your life. Be sure to have your Emotion Wheel and a timer handy because you'll be doing four segments of three minutes in a row. Ideally, you'll do this exercise with a buddy who will sit silently with you to ensure you use all three minutes for each step below:

Step 1. Negative Evaluation State
Have your buddy set the timer for three minutes. During those three minutes, say out loud all the things you don't like about what you're resisting: what's bad about it, what you can't stand about it, how painful it is, how it

makes you feel, why it's wrong. Really trash it. As soon as the three minutes are up, look at the Emotion Wheel and identify your key emotions in this state of Negative Evaluation. Then have your buddy break your state. He or she can invite you to shake your body out, or he or she can ask you a non sequitur question involving a number, such as "How many stripes does a zebra have?" or he or she can ask you to count backward from 10 to 1.

Step 2. Curiosity State

Have your buddy set the timer for three minutes. Now get really curious about this situation. How did it come to be? What is interesting about it? What is familiar about it? What good things come from it? As soon as the three minutes are up, look at the Emotion Wheel and identify your key emotions in this state of Curiosity. Then, have your buddy break your state. He or she can invite you to shake your body out, or he or she can ask you a non sequitur question involving a number, such as "How many spots does a cheetah have?" or he or she can ask you to count backward from 10 to 1.

Step 3. Amazement State

Have your buddy set the timer for three minutes, and now become amazed that this situation came to be. Wow! This is fascinating! What's amazing about it? How do you feel about it? As soon as the three minutes are up, look at the Emotion Wheel and identify your key emotions in this state of Amazement. Then, have your buddy break your state. He or she can invite you to shake your body out, or he or she can ask you a non sequitur question involving a number, such as "How many grains of sand are on perfect beach?" or he or she can ask you to count backward from 10 to 1.

Step 4. Full Appreciation State

Have your buddy set the timer for three minutes. Ahhhh . . . now honor everything about this situation: "Yes! This has been so very helpful in bringing me to the next level. Wow." So much gratitude and appreciation. How do you feel about it as you're honoring it? As soon as the three minutes are up, look at the Emotion Wheel and identify your key emotions in this state of Full Appreciation. Then have your buddy break your state. He or she can invite you to shake your body out, or he or she can ask you a non sequitur question involving a number, such as "What's your favorite number?" or he or she can ask you to count backward from 10 to 1.

Tool: Outcome Frame

Now to ground this new emotional state, let's do a short Outcome Frame. In an Outcome Frame, you create a clear vision of your Desired State (DS) and then bask in it—really see, hear, and feel yourself in your DS—for at least 15 minutes.

We need a clear DS because once you release resistance, you need a *new* trajectory to move toward. Remember, human beings always choose the best available feeling on their menu. Using the Outcome Frame to ground the DS is a way to add more choices to the menu. We'll do a deep dive on this tool in Chapter 6, but for now, answer the following questions to create an Outcome Frame to point the energy you've released from resistance in the right direction:

1. What would you like? Name something you *alone* can create and maintain, something reasonable you can create in a future that isn't too far away, such as more alone time.

2. What will having that do for you? What benefits will you receive? How will you feel? Maybe more relaxed, happier, healthier.

3. How will you know when you have it? What criteria will prove that you got it? How will your world specifically be improved once you have it? For example, you'll have two hours alone outdoors in nature each Saturday and 30 minutes of reading each night.

4. When, where, and with whom would you like it? What is the scope and timing? Do you want it at home, at work, or both?

5. What of value might you risk or lose? Get present to the risk. What might change? What side effects may occur? Is it OK to risk or lose these things? Perhaps you'll have to say no to your family or set healthy boundaries or risk people being disappointed.

6. What are your next steps? Now get into action. What would you put on your to-do list to turn this outcome into reality? You might put recurring time in your calendar and then discuss this with your family and ask for their support.

7. How do you feel now? Grab your Emotion Wheel and notice the experience you are having. What was it like to maneuver

intentionally from resisting to consenting to desiring? Notice how *your experience is what you say it is. Your experience is what you decide it is.* That's how powerful our beliefs are. That's how powerful *you* are.

Now that we understand the role of resistance, the energy of emotions, and how easy it is to change our emotions by maneuvering our consciousness, let's learn how to live more consistently in the emotional state we want.

SUMMARY

1. Resisting your experience is like having your fingers stuck in a Chinese finger trap. The initial reaction of the victim is to resist and pull his or her fingers outward, but this only tightens the trap.

2. To release resistance, we must consent to our Present State (PS) experience. Consent doesn't mean agreeing, accepting, approving, condoning, surrendering, or any other synonyms. It just means to be present with, without any other emotion or judgment attached.

3. You can't release resistance if you are not present to the experience you are currently having. With the Emotion Wheel, you can identify your emotions and release resistance to what you are experiencing.

4. Once you release resistance to your experience, you can use the Maneuvers of Consciousness tool and the Outcome Frame tool to move toward what you desire. To ground your Desired State (DS) and add more choices to your situation, spend at least 15 minutes using the Outcome Frame tool.

TWITTER TAKEAWAYS

• We resist things, situations, or people that we perceive as hurtful, painful, or threatening to our safety, belonging, or mattering.

• To transform resistance, we use the power of consent. That isn't saying something is OK. It is simply acknowledging reality.

- When we are aware of our emotions, we can transform them.

- Whatever we focus on, we fuel. When we resist the emotion, we make it stronger.

- Your experience is what you say it is, what you decide it is. That's how powerful our beliefs are. That's how powerful *you* are.

RESOURCES

See this chapter's section on www.PowerYourTribe.com for the following:

- Chapter *Quick Summary* video

- *Outcome Frame* video

- Organizational Change Path: Understand What's Happening During Change

CHAPTER 4

Increase Rapport with Yourself

To live in a state of emotional agility more consistently, we need to build the mental muscles of self-awareness. We do so by increasing emotional rapport with ourself and stilling the constant chatter of the mind.

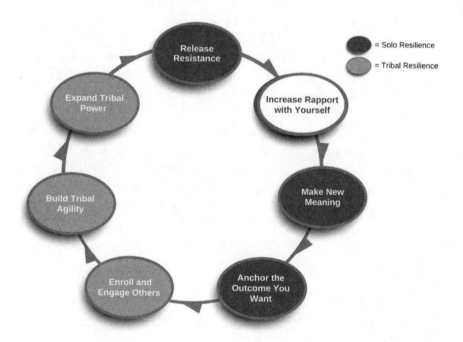

Figure 4.1 The Resilience Cycle: Increase Rapport with Yourself

PROBLEM

Tania is a brilliant CEO of a super successful accounting firm. Carlos, her VP of operations, is a bright and solid asset to the firm. But sometimes Tania and Carlos clash big time, especially when Tania wants faster results and shorter timelines on client projects. Then Carlos slows down—fast results to him mean poor quality and possible problems in client care, which he also owns. So as Carlos gets more cautious, Tania gets more impatient and massively triggered. She feels unsafe and starts to micromanage Carlos, who then rebels, feels unappreciated, and grinds to a halt. He will not make a client-facing mistake. Period.

Tania and Carlos want the same thing: high-quality work delivered to clients in a timely manner. But they both have needs that they need to tune in to: Tania's is safety, and Carlos's is safety and mattering. When Carlos's needs aren't honored, he cannot take action. When Tania's needs aren't honored, she feels devalued. As a result, projects are delayed, and unhappy clients call Tania, who then gets more upset. She and Carlos lose even more trust in each other, and Tania feels unsafe selling more client engagements because what if they are delivered late?

The team gets confused and thinks, "Wait a sec! We have these huge leaderboards showing our sales, quality, and client deliverable deadlines. So why are we selling less? Delivering late? Questioning quality?" Half of the team goes into panic and fight or flight, while the other half freezes. They're all in Critter State.

This scenario is a perfect example of the big negative repercussions a business can experience when leaders' needs aren't honored. Although Carlos and Tania wanted the same thing, their individual needs were slightly different, and they made different negative meaning when these conflicts arose. As a result, client relationships were at risk, the team lost confidence and panicked, and the drive for sales decreased.

PROMISE

What happens inside you when someone you're counting on drops the ball? Do you crave safety as Carlos does? Or safety and mattering as Tania does? Or something else?

For Tania to become more emotionally agile, she needed to first identify the core "right" she felt she didn't have that was throwing fuel on the behavioral fire. Next, she needed to get in touch with the "part" of her having the emotional reaction that was leading to the behavior of micromanaging and ultimately alienating Carlos. Finally, she needed to raise her overall behavioral baseline (which at that moment was in the most negative feeling state) so that she could gradually respond from choice rather than compulsively reacting when a trigger event occurred. That way, Tania could create an environment where she experienced more control, confidence, and support—in comparison to her Present State of chaos in which her tendency was toward excessive control and constantly mistrusting Carlos.

To achieve this, we needed to determine which Organismic Rights she felt weren't being met. *Organismic Rights* are our basic human rights that are established during our early life experiences. They determine where a person will have behavioral struggles as he or she moves through life. Put simply, like all of us, Tania had her own set of "growth areas" to work on. They were governing her behavior and hindering her performance—and she was totally unaware of them.

We then used the *Parts Process* to establish rapport with the part of her that was causing the painful behavior. Then we helped her set up a regular routine of using *Mindfulness Practices* to increase and maintain rapport (establishing safety, belonging, and mattering) with herself.

We did the same with Carlos.

Until Tania and Carlos were appreciated as human beings doing the best they could, they would continually be triggered by each other, and the business would suffer.

RESULT

Once Tania got in touch with the part of herself that felt abandoned (the K– of feeling abandoned) when others did not behave as she wanted (the Vs and As that let her know she was invisible, which led to the K– of feeling abandoned), she was able to add some new choices to her behavioral menu in this scenario.

Tania's main belief about herself (identity) was "I'm all alone." So she often put others' needs before hers and was unwilling to accept help. With this new understanding and self-awareness, she could start setting healthy boundaries and communicate her needs very specifically to Carlos.

We added new options and feelings to her emotional menu: feeling *supported* and feeling *safe* enough to reach for support. These were the new best available K+s on her menu. And these helped her create *new meaning*. If you recall, the prefrontal cortex of the brain combines new sets of sensory information (Vs and As) from the reptilian brain with the feelings from the mammalian brain (K+) to create new meaning and beliefs.

With Tania's clearer communication and new written agreements with all department leaders (including Carlos), Carlos could also rise to a new level of communication and flexibility. Carlos wanted to be safe, which led to his feeling of belonging with the tribe, so once the impact of his putting on the brakes became clearer, his behavior started to change. He learned that he procrastinated at times due to his own lower experience of the specific Organismic Rights of taking action and having consequences (we'll talk more about these later in the chapter).

The end result was a deeper, more respectful relationship between Tania and Carlos, as well as far less stress for their direct reports who had been suffering the consequences of the prior behavioral dynamic.

Which relationships at work and at home would benefit from greater understanding of each other? Think about these individuals as you learn these next tools.

We've learned about our Critter State and how we all have hijacking or self-sabotaging behavior. We've also learned that emotions have energy, as measured by Dr. Hawkins. We have an Emotion Wheel to decode how we're feeling at any given time, and if we find we're resisting our Present State, we can use the Maneuvers of Consciousness and Outcome Frame tools to shift our experience.

Now let's add some tools to help us shift the *grooves of meaning* that keep us stuck. These *grooves* are the consistent behavior patterns that may not serve us, yet we find ourselves repeating them incessantly, as if we were stuck in a groove on an old long-playing (LP) record. Shifting these grooves of meaning will help you further expand your identity in the Logical Levels of Change, increase your behavioral choices, and more easily and automatically shift from resistance to consent.

THE FIVE ORGANISMIC RIGHTS: CLAIMING YOUR RIGHTS AS A HUMAN BEING

Imagine a newborn baby entering the world. He or she is forced to adapt quickly. The psychoanalyst Wilhelm Reich observed a series of stages through which all human beings must pass on their way to full body maturation, referred to as *Organismic Rights*.[1] The more fully developed they are, the more that individuals can express themselves with greater aliveness and creativity (Smart State). The less developed, the more likely they will operate in the Critter State.

The Five Organismic Rights are these:

1. The right to exist

2. The right to have needs

3. The right to take action

4. The right to have consequences for one's actions

5. The right to love and be loved

Table 4.1 is a very rough Organismic Rights behavior decoder tool, and it is based on my experience of working over 10,000 hours with humans on changing their behavior.

Note that you can use this on yourself or with others too. For example, if people are struggling with accountability, they may need help increasing their right to take action. If they often blame others for their shortcomings, they may need help with the right of having consequences.

TABLE 4.1 Organismic Rights Behavior Decoder

Organismic Right	Behavior in Critter State	What You Might Crave	How You Can Shift into Smart State	How You Can Help Another Shift into Smart State
To exist	If a person plays small, keeps their head down, tries to be invisible, or becomes silent in times of conflict, chances are they don't experience having the right to exist.	Safety, mattering	Acknowledging yourself and letting yourself be seen by proactively communicating and participating, intentionally taking a role.	Acknowledging them, including them, giving them a role.

Organismic Right	Behavior in Critter State	What You Might Crave	How You Can Shift into Smart State	How You Can Help Another Shift into Smart State
To have needs	If a person frequently puts others' needs before their own, self-sacrifices, "takes one for the team" repeatedly, or doesn't actually know what they want, chances are they don't experience having the right to have needs.	Mattering, belonging	Being present and asking for what you need specifically, letting people know what you can't do, setting healthy boundaries, saying no when tempted to overextend yourself.	Helping out, showing you're in this together, sharing the workload.
To take action	If a person often procrastinates or avoids commitment, chances are good they don't experience having the right to take action.	Safety, mattering	Getting an accountability partner to support you in making and keeping commitments, making sure you understand what "success" is so you can take action and move forward.	Help them form a plan, pair them up with an action-oriented person.
To have consequences for actions	If a person often uses victim language, blames others for their own choices and actions, or avoids accountability, chances are good they don't experience having the right to have consequences.	Belonging, mattering	Think of how others are impacted by your choices, consider what potential outcomes could be, look carefully at your role in what you create in your life.	Explain that course-correction is how we learn and make things better, map out the best case/ worst case/likely case scenarios, and commit to helping them work through each.

Organismic Right	Behavior in Critter State	What You Might Crave	How You Can Shift into Smart State	How You Can Help Another Shift into Smart State
To love and be loved	If a person is uncomfortable with giving or receiving affection or being around theirs or others' deep hurt or emotion, chances are good they don't experience having the right to love or be loved.	Belonging, safety	Ask for affection, ensure you reach out to friends/ family, practice staying present when people around you emote, consider the benefits of compassion versus empathy.	Use the Emotion Wheel to help them understand what they are feeling, help them use Maneuvers of Consciousness to shift to Desired State.

Now that you see how certain behaviors may reveal some minimal Organismic Rights, please take a moment to review your own life (particularly where you most often get stuck, stressed, or self-sabotaged) and rate each of the rights above on a scale of 0 to 5, where 0 means you feel you have no right and 5 means you feel you have the full total right:

1. Your right to exist: _____

2. Your right to have needs: _____

3. Your right to take action: _____

4. Your right to have consequences for your actions: _____

5. Your right to love and be loved: _____

Consider your ratings. Where would you like to increase your rights? Where do you think your stakeholders at work stand? Your family members?

When we can't say something is not OK, our Organismic Rights are threatened. It's OK, and essential, to claim our Organismic Rights to exist, have needs, take action, have consequences for our actions, and love and be loved. When we are told (explicitly or implicitly) that having any of these rights is *not* OK, our entire humanity is being dismissed. Let's take a sec and let that sink in. It's big.

To honor our Organismic Rights; to be safe, belong, and matter; and to engage all three parts of our brain—for all of these to occur, we already know that we need to be honest about our emotions, and we need to consent to our Present State. The tricky part is when our Organismic Rights aren't being honored. When we are stuck, stressed, or sabotaged, we often will default to resistance—which, as we already know, requires a ton of energy. Does resistance work, ultimately? No. It just keeps us stuck fighting our Present State rather than helping us create our Desired State.

How do we choose to honor our Organismic Rights when we're already in Critter State and stuck in resistance? That brings us to our next tool, the Parts Process.

THE PARTS PROCESS: ESTABLISH RAPPORT WITH ALL YOUR PARTS

Most of us habitually do things we wish we didn't. In the moment, we might even excuse ourselves by naming other things we are doing that are good. For example: "It's OK that I'm having this donut. That was a tough client call, I did well, and I deserve it." But at some point, usually not too long after eating the donut, we acknowledge that shoving a ball of fat and fast carbs into our mouth is really not the best thing for us.

Unfortunately, we often try to change these self-sabotaging habits by fighting ourselves. We beat ourselves up, make New Year's resolutions, think of ourselves as weak—and hope that the "good guy" wins. But as Carl Buchheit says in his article "10 Delusions of Personal Growth": "If one part of us wins over another part of us, who is it exactly who's won?"[2]

The key to remember when transforming self-sabotage is this: the behavior you dislike was once a solution. And not just any solution—it was the absolute best solution you had at the time. Behavior always, always, always has an *intended positive outcome* (IPO). But the method of achieving that outcome (the behavior) simply got locked in early in life and is now outdated.

Instead of fighting self-sabotage, let's learn to transform it by befriending—establishing rapport with—the part of you who came up with the solution in the first place.

Let's start by calling it something different. Instead of calling it "my horrible donut habit" or "self-sabotage" or something derogatory, rename it as a part of you that represents something positive, solution oriented, or at least neutral. I call the part of me that needs recuperation time "my sensitive self." If I want donuts or junk food or I am overwhelmed and grumpy, it's often because my sensitive self is feeling a bit crumpled or trodden on.

And the thing is, I love my sensitive self. It's the part of me that excels at compassion. It's the part of me that understands others best. That's why I'm good at what I do. So I've given my sensitive self a voice, a new methodology to get me some respite instead of reaching for the cookie jar or lashing out. It tells me when I need to take a bath, enforce a boundary, go to bed early, or recall my energy in other ways.

The intended positive outcome is the same—protection—but by honoring that part and by not making it wrong, by giving it a voice and listening to it, I can choose different methods to get that same outcome of protection and soothing.

The Parts Model

Having a deeper rapport with yourself means having a grateful congruence between what you want to do and what you actually do. Deeper rapport with yourself means greater understanding of why you do what you do. Deeper rapport with yourself means greater compassion, connection, and kindness with yourself.

Question: Does a part of you want one thing while a different part wants the opposite? Of course. You are human. Heck, I frequently talk about doing cardio every day, but a few days per week, a part of me just isn't up for it.

You have many parts to your subconscious mind. You created these parts from the moment you were born in order to navigate life, to deal with challenges, to survive, to be safe, to belong, to matter.

The Parts Model was established as early as 1976 by Richard Bandler and John Grinder, two of the pioneers of neurolinguistics.[3] This model will help you establish deeper rapport with yourself and all of your parts. You can begin by using it to reconnect with your disenfranchised, rebellious, and self-sabotaging parts, and over time you can use it also to establish deeper collaboration among the many parts of your subconscious mind.

The premises of the Parts Model are these:

- Human beings often have conflicting opinions or ideas about something.

- Human beings often do and are what they say they don't want to do or be.

- Human beings often don't do and aren't what they say they *do* want to do or want to be.

- Human beings don't like to be wrong or feel stupid.

There are eight main assumptions in the Parts Model:

1. People have parts.

2. Parts are created by people in response to their experiences in life, often to deal with particular tasks, contexts, or events.

3. Parts can agree or disagree both among themselves and with the "senior consciousness" (the human being) whom they serve.

4. Parts are loyal and brilliantly creative, but they are also supremely literal.

5. Parts are never willing to let go of or relinquish their purpose.

6. Parts can never be fired, yet they can always be promoted.

7. Parts *always* operate from a positive intention. There are no exceptions to this. None. Not ever.

8. Parts have no sense of time.

Have you ever labeled someone as a "problem person" or "problem employee"? If so, it was probably because the person had a negative behavior—destructive, ineffective, you name it. And as you focused on the problem person, did you happen to notice that you saw more and more evidence of how problematic the person was?

When you label people as the problem, they are limited in their choice to do something about it because *they* are identified as the problem.

However, if you relate to those people as people who have problematic *behavior* in a certain context, then those people can do something to change their behavior. They have a choice.

Remember, humans are good. It's just that our behaviors at times can be challenging in that they result in our not getting what we want, causing harm to self and others, and more unpleasantness. Let's pause for a moment and consider this. By separating the person from the behavior, we can address the behavior without condemning the person.

As Wayne Dyer said, what we focus on, we notice. Add to this the fact that our brains delete, distort, and generalize, and boom—some people look really problematic because our brains are deleting all the good things they may actually be doing, possibly distorting the impact of what they are doing, and generalizing that they are always a hassle. The Parts Model helps us to see that all challenging behaviors serve a useful purpose at some level. This purpose is almost always unconscious, and it has a positive intention. (A positive intention is the "good thing" your part hopes to get from the behavior.) Using this Parts Model, we can turn obstacles into opportunities. We can use the challenge of change to power our tribe.

For example, a while back we had a CEO come to us for coaching. He frequently screamed at his team when he was highly stressed. This resulted, not surprisingly, in a revolving door of executives at his organization. I was curious about what the positive intention was, what good his system wanted to get from the screaming behavior. First, I led him through an Outcome Frame (see Chapter 3) to ensure that changing this behavior would be safe and acceptable (particularly question 5, "What of value might you risk or lose?"). Would he survive without this screaming behavior? Or had he "coded" screaming under stress to equal survival?

Using the Parts Process tool that follows, I quickly learned that the positive intention was indeed survival. At two years old, he learned that screaming was how he got his most basic needs met. It was an appropriate behavior for a two-year-old in a chaotic, often unpredictable home where his needs would be ignored were he quiet. But at age 53, the behavior of screaming wasn't appropriate. It was causing too much damage to both himself and the organization, and it would be best if replaced with a new behavior that still ensured that our client's most basic needs would be met and he would indeed survive.

By distinguishing between behavior and intention, we can understand, appreciate, and adjust behaviors without judgment. This is key. And by discovering that every part of us has a positive intention—regardless of the current behavior—we build a solid foundation for self-trust.

This process enables us to acquire new behavior choices that are more congruent with the true intention of the part that is generating the behavior. The unwanted behavior was once deeply wanted—it is simply an old solution that has outstayed its welcome.

Tool: Parts Process

The Parts Process tool has four steps as given below.

Step 1. Define the Present State

What exactly is the behavior that's not working? Get very clear in your mind what the trigger is (what happens before the problem behavior), what you specifically do as a result (the problem behavior), and what happens during and afterward. How is each useful? How is it not?

For example, let's say you are staying up late zoning out in front of the TV on weeknights when you have to get up early. Notice exactly what happens *before* you start watching TV. Are you tired to begin with and TV feels soothing and rebellious? Does going to bed early require effort and maybe feels like succumbing to a different—less cool—version of yourself? Hmm. Maybe the "staying up late behavior" does not actually support your best you.

Step 2. Find the Part Responsible

Take a few deep breaths and let your body lie back or sit back. Close your eyes. Set the intention for all of your parts to gather in an auditorium or other venue in your mind's eye. Your parts can be like little personalities on their own, with names and opinions. You created this part to help you achieve a specific positive outcome (even a seemingly vindictive part always has an IPO—possibly to feel good or be safe).

Then let the part of you that is responsible for the behavior come into your awareness. Ask the part directly, "What do you wish for me to have or accomplish by doing this behavior?"

Step 3. Establish the Part's Core Motive (Its Intended Positive Outcome)

Keep asking the part "what" and "why" questions until you're clear. Often the answers track back to safety and self-love. Release any judgment.

Remember, this behavior was the best solution a younger you had. Let the part know you'll never fire it. You created that part to achieve something important, and it's been doing a great job. Once you are clear on the IPO, you can negotiate with the part about using a different methodology.

In our late-night TV example, the IPO might be self-expression (perhaps a teenage version of yourself that learned to watch TV late to cope with fatigue from the demands of school and parents and still have a sense of self and behavior choice).

Step 4. Ask the Part If It Would Be Willing to Update Its Method

You can offer some suggestions, bring in wise or creative parts, or just leave it to the part. Be really clear about how the method isn't working (from step 1). Keep working with the part and honoring the IPO until you reach agreement. In our example, the part might receive a promotion. It's now in charge of getting you to bed and adding a creative spice to your life (a different method to achieve the IPO of self-expression).

• • •

It is easier to respond to the intention of a behavior rather than the problem. It also helps us to groove our brains in useful ways.

Try it! You'll be surprised to find out how hard those parts of yours that "sabotage" you are actually working, however misguidedly, on your behalf. I use a very detailed version of the above tool when coaching clients who want to increase rapport with themselves around a certain behavior. It takes a good 45 minutes or longer, so give yourself a chunk of time to go through the steps.

In addition to increasing rapport with all our parts, another way to increase choice of our emotional state is to enhance our ability to *self-regulate*, which is our ability to choose not to send that flaming e-mail when we're angry, for example. Self-regulation is the ability to note that things aren't entirely cool right now, so we can take a time-out and reassess what we want, blow off steam, or do something else. One of the best ways to increase self-regulation is to practice *mindfulness*, which leads us to the final tool.

MINDFULNESS MEDITATION: DECREASE REPETITIVE THOUGHTS AND INCREASE BEHAVIORAL CHOICE

What stresses you out? We all have situations in which it is harder to maintain equilibrium than it is in others. Mine is having to do too many administrative tasks that should be done by someone else. What's yours?

In these situations, we know we "shouldn't" get freaked out and anxious, we know staying present will enable us to find better solutions, we know we "should" be getting a good night's rest to tackle the situation with a fresh mind the next day, but we can't always get there without help. We've been hijacked. Our patterns are in charge. We're human.

One of the greatest indicators of my clients' success in stepping up their leadership is whether they have an existing mindfulness practice or are willing to start one.

Mindfulness meditation has long been touted as an effective way to improve our health and well-being, but studies have been notoriously subjective and difficult to validate. New studies from top institutions such as Harvard, Johns Hopkins, and Yale are reporting tangible and measurable benefits, such as improved concentration, improved focus and attention, less stress and anxiety, greater productivity, stronger leadership, more peaceful and fulfilling lives, more happiness, more energy, and better sleep.[4] (For more on the latest research, visit www.PowerYourTribe.com.)

The Mind Is a Lousy Master . . . and an Excellent Servant

How exactly does mindfulness meditation help us? One of the biggest causes of stress is ruminating, or repeating a certain stressful thought. The brain sets off down an old thinking pattern and stays there—causing continued Critter State and painful feelings. According to the research of the late great Dr. Wayne Dyer, a human being has approximately 60,000 thoughts *per day*—and 90 percent of these are repetitive![5]

Mindfulness practices teach our brain to pop out of that old pattern and recognize it for what it is: a default and well-worn groove that we have a choice to step out of. We have repetitive thoughts because most of us haven't trained our minds to be still. When we train our minds, we get more choice about our responses, our behaviors, and the meaning we make, and we also are able to edit our "grooves of meaning" more effectively (which you'll learn how to do in Chapter 5).

Mindfulness meditation regrooves the brain and builds a new neurological network. Do it enough, and as the studies show, you can train your brain like a muscle to stay calm and present in the face of adversity or the good old daily stresses of life. Then no matter what happens outside of you, you'll more easily get to choose the meaning you make about it inside. More empowering meaning equals more choice, which equals more happiness, which equals a better experience (K+) for yourself and others.

And in *Power Your Tribe* terms, it helps us increase rapport with ourselves, experience greater levels of Organismic Rights, expand our identity in the Logical Levels of Change, and therefore experience greater behavioral choice in stressful situations.

Tool: Mindfulness Meditation

There are many meditation teachers, books, and audio recordings to show you the way. Here are some of my favorite techniques for beginners.

Mindful Breathing

If you've never meditated before, a simple way to start is to breathe in to the count of seven, hold for a count of seven, and exhale for a count of seven. Then repeat. When you're counting, use the "one one thousand, two one thousand, three one thousand . . ." method. If your mind starts to wander, gently bring it back to focus on your breath. Set a timer for five minutes before you start. I recommend sitting upright with palms facing up.

If you want to close your eyes, or light a candle, or place a flower in front of you to focus on, do it. When you're starting out, you're just exploring and finding out what works for you. If you're having a stressful day at the office, practice the above breathing technique. You can even do it during a meeting!

That's why meditation is referred to as a "practice," as in "I'm practicing meditation" or "I have a meditation practice." You're teaching your brain to interrupt repetitive patterns and to calm and center itself. It takes practice to get to automation, but it's worth it.

To further still your mind and regulate your emotional state, here are two more detailed mindfulness meditation practices. All of these practices are helpful for insomnia too. Simply do them in bed as you are lying awake.

Pre-practice prep: Turn off all phones and other noisemakers. Make sure that your family, colleagues, and others cannot disturb you. Sit up straight, whether in a chair or cross-legged. You may want to set a timer for 5 minutes. If you practice mindfulness meditation daily for only 5 minutes, you will see and feel a difference in 30 days or less. I find 30 minutes each morning is ideal.

News Feed

Imagine a news feed across the bottom of a TV screen. There's a bit of news, some white space, then more news, and so on. Your thoughts are like the news. There's always more! Now consider the white space between the thoughts. In Japanese, the word *ma* is loosely translated to mean "pause"— the pause between notes, the pause between breaths, the pause between sentences, the pause between thoughts.

Close your eyes. Place your inner focus on the constant stream of thoughts scrolling across the TV of your mind. See the scrolling thoughts floating in space or actually moving across a screen, whatever image works for you.

Don't pay attention to the thoughts in detail. Let them scroll by. Do not cling to them or reject them. Now focus on the space between the thoughts, the *ma*, the pause. As you focus on the white space between the thoughts, you'll find it getting wider, longer, bigger. In time you'll see mostly emptiness, with few if any thoughts.

Focusing on the *ma*, the pause, the emptiness is a nice practice during the day too. Stop and notice open space as conversations pause, as music pauses. We are surrounded by pauses. That's where some of the best stuff is. We often fill our minds and schedules out of fear of emptiness. Yet emptiness is where true peace, connectedness, and love are found.

Brain Dump

Back in the mainframe computing days, a "core dump" was when the memory and all buffers of the computer were "dumped," or emptied. The result was pages and pages of gibberish as the buffers were flushed. Doing a "core dump" of your mind can be helpful when you have a constant swirl of thoughts or if you're really agitated.

Here's how to do it:

1. Go to a quiet place where you will not be disturbed. Turn off any phones, noisemakers, and other distractions. Have a piece of paper and pen ready.

2. Light a candle (if available) and ask for the highest good for yourself and all beings.

3. Set a timer for 20 minutes.

4. Now start writing about any issue you are obsessing about, want to clear from your mind, want to understand or be free from, or have a question about. Just write, unedited and unpunctuated. When the sheet is full, turn it over, and when that side's full, keep writing upside down, sideways, and so on. You will not be reading this later, so there's no point in using more than one sheet of paper. The only purpose is to keep writing until the timer sounds.

When the time is up, either burn the piece of paper or tear it up and flush it down the toilet. Wash your hands and change your physiology (for example, jump up and down for a moment or roll your shoulders).

You'll find even more mindfulness practices on www.PowerYourTribe. com under the section for this chapter.

Ideally, you'll do a mindfulness meditation practice in the morning to start your day and also in the evening when ending it (or ending work). Notice the tremendous and enduring stillness it creates inside of you. This stillness is where the answers to many of our questions come from. And with this increased ability to get still, it's a lot easier to make new, more empowering meaning about what happens to us. Choosing the meaning we assign to our experiences is essential to create new beliefs and become emotionally agile, and it's what you'll learn next in Chapter 5.

SUMMARY

1. Every behavior has a positive intention behind it. When it is honored for its intended positive outcome (IPO) and the solution it provided in the past, and it is not judged as wrong, the behavior can be adjusted.

2. Most people try to change self-sabotaging habits by fighting themselves. But if we try to change ourselves by arm wrestling ourselves, who wins? No one. Recognize that the behavior you dislike was actually once a useful solution.

3. The Parts Process tool is a great way to deepen rapport with yourself and to experience greater congruence between what you want to do and the behavior that gets you there—especially when the behavior seems destructive, rebellious, and self-sabotaging.

4. It is useful to distinguish the behavior from the person demonstrating the behavior. By separating the person from the behavior, we can address the behavior without condemning the person—empowering the person with more choice.

5. According to Wilhelm Reich, we have five Organismic Rights as humans: the right to exist, have needs, take action, have consequences for our actions, and love and be loved. When any of these rights are denied or violated, our humanity is being dismissed.

6. Mindfulness practices have been proven to increase brain function and to help us stay calm no matter what happens externally. They're a key tool for getting into your Smart State and staying there.

TWITTER TAKEAWAYS

- Key to remember when transforming self-sabotage: The behavior you dislike was once a solution.

- Behavior always, always, always has an intended positive outcome (IPO).

- By separating the person from the behavior, we can address the behavior without condemning the person.

- More empowering meaning = more choice = more happiness = a better experience for yourself and others.

- Choosing the meaning we assign to our experiences is essential to creating new beliefs and being emotionally agile.

RESOURCES

See this chapter's section on www.PowerYourTribe.com for the following:

- Chapter *Quick Summary* video

- More mindfulness practices

- Latest mindfulness research

- *Gratitude Practice* video

- *Five-Minute Mindfulness* video

- *Mindfulness in Leadership* video

CHAPTER 5

Make New Meaning

Shakespeare was right: nothing is good or bad but thinking makes it so. Learn how to choose your response to what happens to you and the story you want to tell about it.

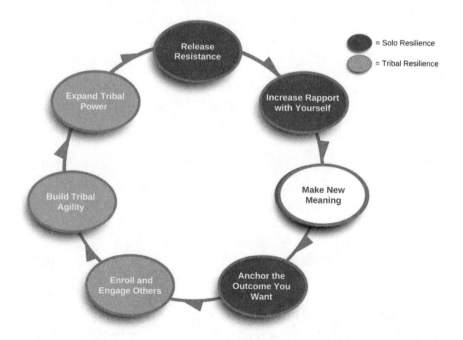

Figure 5.1 The Resilience Cycle: Make New Meaning

PROBLEM

The engineering team of a software organization was in a challenging situation—one that many of their competitors envied. Their users had rapidly risen to 10 million, and growth was teetering on the edge of out of control. Their well-loved chief strategist had just jumped ship for a seven-figure compensation package after a grueling seven years of struggle with the organization's well-meaning but often meddling founder. Now the engineers were discouraged, grieving the loss of their leader, feeling betrayed, and also fearful of what the founder would do.

Would the engineers now be reporting to him? Or would he recruit a new leader for them? Without a trusted, wise leader, how could they keep up with the relentless demand for new features? And who would push back when the founder asked for too much?

The engineering team didn't see that it was *they* who had built the amazing software—not the chief strategist. Also, the strategy had been laid out for the next year, and they knew what they had to do to make it work. Sure, they needed a few more people and someone to negotiate with the founder, but they had all the skills they needed to develop, maintain, and optimize great software.

PROMISE

Have you ever had a key and well-loved leader leave? What was the impact on your team? In times like these, people usually tell scary stories about the future.

First, via executive coaching, we worked with the founder to identify an interim leader and collectively to forge a code of conduct. The founder could contribute his feature suggestions, but a three-person team (engineering, sales, marketing) would determine which features made it into a given release.

Next, we had to dial down the disempowering thinking by shining some light on everyone's internal process. In a group coaching session, we used our *Distorted Thinking Decoder* so the engineers could state individually and openly which distortion they were suffering from. This helped them drain the distortion's power. We also had to let people grieve the loss of their leader and not pretend it wasn't a big painful deal. Then we had the interim leader start using *Neuro Storytelling* to help the team form a new, more expansive, and powerful set of beliefs and to help them reframe—to make new meaning about—the challenges they were facing.

RESULT

Fast-forward six months and the engineering team was on fire—they were a well-synchronized, lean mean coding machine. They supported one another in editing their beliefs on a regular basis, and the interim leader did such a great job helping the team pivot that she became the new chief strategist.

Now and then a team will suffer a loss, but that's OK because they still have the recipe to get them back on track. Going forward, they can forge their new team together. They can navigate their grief together. They can succeed together.

REFRAMING: CHANGE THE STORY, CHANGE THE MEANING

As you learned in Part I, we form our own reality based on visual, auditory, and kinesthetic cues. These cues recall our beliefs about the world and ourselves (our identity), which results in either feeling good or feeling bad. If you're on a sales team that feels bad, chances are you won't be achieving your quota because your energy will be low as well as your motivation and creativity. Is there anything you can do right now to feel better *and* be more productive?

Stuff happens, and sometimes we need to do a quick "pattern-interrupt" to pause our default and choose a better-feeling alternative. Remember, it is not what happens that matters but rather what it *means* that matters. Change the meaning, change the feeling. We need to make more helpful meaning.

In the last chapter, you learned how mindfulness meditation can help you interrupt repetitive thought patterns and create new grooves of thinking. This sets you up to make new and more helpful meaning. And *reframing* is a terrific tool for making new meaning quickly and easily, as well as for editing your belief system in the process.

By formal definition, reframing is a way of viewing and experiencing events, ideas, concepts, and emotions to find more useful alternatives. It is a practical and valuable tool to shift perception, including your perception of yourself or others' perceptions of themselves.

Think of reframing as putting on a different pair of glasses. What would you see if you put on a pair of sunglasses with a heavy tint when you were in a dark room? You would see shadows and dark forms you couldn't identify. What would happen when you took off those glasses? You may see the most beautiful room in the world. When you switch your glasses, what you see changes. Reframing, mentally and linguistically, does the same thing. It changes the story you tell yourself about what happens.

Harvard researchers proved a while back that the stories we tell ourselves shape our world.[1] The good news is that we can also create new stories—the decisions we've made about ourselves, our abilities, and the world—and change our experience. Here are two examples.

In Business

Initial story: It's really hard getting a job fresh out of college these days. The market is crowded, and overqualified people are competing for every single job. No wonder I'm unemployed—it's tough.

Reframe: It's awesome that there are a lot of people job hunting right now because it gives a person the opportunity to really bring his or her "A Game" to stand out. I'm sending my résumé in creative ways to get an interview, I'm doing more research than I ever have done before to prepare for interviews, and then I'm following up after the interviews using different methods. I am learning a ton!

See how the meaning shifts from defeat and deciding that job hunting will be hard (which means it will be because the universe is an exquisite mirror) to a sense of power, can-do, creativity, and agility?

In Personal Life

Initial story: I was a girl in a household of boys. My brothers and parents wanted another boy, so I was perpetually left out and labeled as a disappointment. I've never been good enough.

Reframe: I grew up in the perfect family to learn to see and honor my unique value. I was given great opportunities to be independent and forge my path in life. I also learned to be self-reliant, which has made me strong and fearless.

See how the meaning she is making shifts from disempowering to empowering?

Although the tools that follow (the Distorted Thinking Decoder and Neuro Storytelling) will help you reframe your situation, you can also reframe all sorts of scenarios daily. Here's how it works.

Tool: Reframing

Imagine your spouse has just made the morning coffee. While scooping the grounds into the coffee machine, he or she has spilled a considerable amount on the counter. He or she doesn't notice this and moves on to the next item in the morning routine. You could focus on the "bad" behavior, complain about the mess, start a fight, and have no coffee or affection that morning. Or you could practice reframing in one of at least two ways:

1. **Context reframing:** These reframes work on the principle that every behavior is useful in some context. So when we change the context, we also change the meaning we make about another's behavior. In this spilled coffee example, you could use a context reframe as follows: "Your spilling coffee means we are so much more privileged than 80 percent of the world who can't afford to have coffee with breakfast!" This is exaggerated, yes, but it illustrates how drastically the meaning can change when you expand and change the context.

2. **Content reframing:** Content reframes work by changing the actual content of the meaning you give the behavior. In the spilled coffee example, a content reframe might be, "Your spilling coffee doesn't mean you made a mess. It just means you were rushing to make sure I was taken care of."

The behavior and the facts of the matter are the same; we've just altered our self-talk to make different meaning from the coffee grounds on the counter. And after all, at the end of the day, do you care more about some coffee grounds or about your relationship? In the same way, which do you care more about in business: success as a team or blame and shame?

Tool: Distorted Thinking Decoder

Sometimes a whole team can be stuck in a cycle of negative distorted thinking. That means it's time for a group reframe and some collective new meaning making!

Recall from Chapter 2 that the brain naturally and usefully deletes, distorts, and generalizes information. It's necessary for survival because without this capability, we would simply be overwhelmed with input. However, occasionally these distortions can get grooved into a not-so-useful pattern. Look out for some common distortions listed in what we affectionately refer to as the *Distorted Thinking Decoder* (Table 5.1). Here's how to use this tool:

TABLE 5.1 Distorted Thinking Decoder

Always or never	You swing to extremes of expecting something to always or never be a certain way: "It will always be this way, or it will never work out."
Generalization	You decide one data point has a certain meaning: "Pointing means the person is rude." Now all people who point are rude.
Deletion or denial	You choose to delete information that doesn't serve you or that would cause you discomfort: "So what if she doesn't return my calls? I still know she digs me."
Assumption	You assume that something will happen or be true based on limited data: "He said he agreed with our approach, so I'm sure he'll sign off on the budget."
Distortion	You blow things out of proportion after a challenging experience: "I'll never date again!" or "My life is ruined!"
Identification	You identify with something outside yourself as yourself: "My report wasn't well received so I am useless."

1. Look through the table. Which distortions are most potent for you? For your team? For your organizational culture?

2. For each distortion, name the meaning that is being made from a behavior or circumstance. Think of it like an equation: in our minds, this behavior (or circumstance) = something negative.

3. Try replacing the negative with something positive and/or empowering. Inside your head, say to yourself, "That [behavior or circumstance] doesn't mean [something bad]. It means [something positive]!" This is what reframing is all about.

For example, let's say there's a lot of labeling going on, and someone who made a mistake is a "careless loser." Try applying the thinking, "What if that behavior (making a mistake) meant something positive?" In this case, you could try, "Making a mistake means someone is trying new things. That person is innovating and learning." Look for some evidence to back up this new meaning. Then try saying it to others about a particular incident.

Make a game out of shifting the team out of distortions that are pulling you and others into Critter State. Using the reframe you came up with in this exercise, try saying it to as many people as possible in a morning. Then sit back and watch it go around just like a game of telephone. The words will shift, but the intention won't. Also note that distorted thinking often occurs due to cognitive biases, which we'll learn about in Chapter 8.

NEURO STORYTELLING: SHIFT MEANING QUICKLY WITH A GREAT STORY

One of the best ways to help teams reframe is via storytelling. It allows you to change your stance, make new meaning, and shift your team out of the *Tension Triangle* (victim, rescuer, persecutor) and into the *Empowerment Triangle* (outcome creator, insight creator, action creator).[2]

We've all seen corporate mission, vision, and value statements that are simply wall art and devoid of emotion. They're not memorable.

Why? There's no story.

What's your favorite movie? I'll bet you can enthusiastically tell me all about it even if you haven't seen it in years. Stories are like nutrition for our souls. We remember them and love them. They have deeper meaning for us. On YouTube, there's a wonderful video clip of a group of marines belting out the lyrics to the theme song from Disney's *Frozen*.[3] Who would have thought combat soldiers could relate to a Disney princess?

And then there are stories of exceptional organizations. Many of us have heard the story about a Nordstrom's customer returning a snow tire, and the customer service rep handling that request happily, even though Nordstrom doesn't sell snow tires. We don't need to be told that Nordstrom values customer service. We know; we have the story.

People love to tell stories; they are potent engagement and teaching tools. They help us to navigate change by experiencing it vicariously through the characters in the story.

Notice what makes stories memorable for you. For most people, the stories we remember have some sort of emotional impact on us. They have this impact because we can relate to the hero and the story line in some way. The stories you tell about your organization need to be positively impactful too. *Neural coupling* enables us to connect to the story and personalize it (Figure 5.2). We connect to the storyteller via mirror neurons; we get deeply engaged and feel, hear, and see and even smell or taste what's happening in the story. Dopamine, a feel-good neurotransmitter, is released when a story is emotionally engaging. And that's just a start!

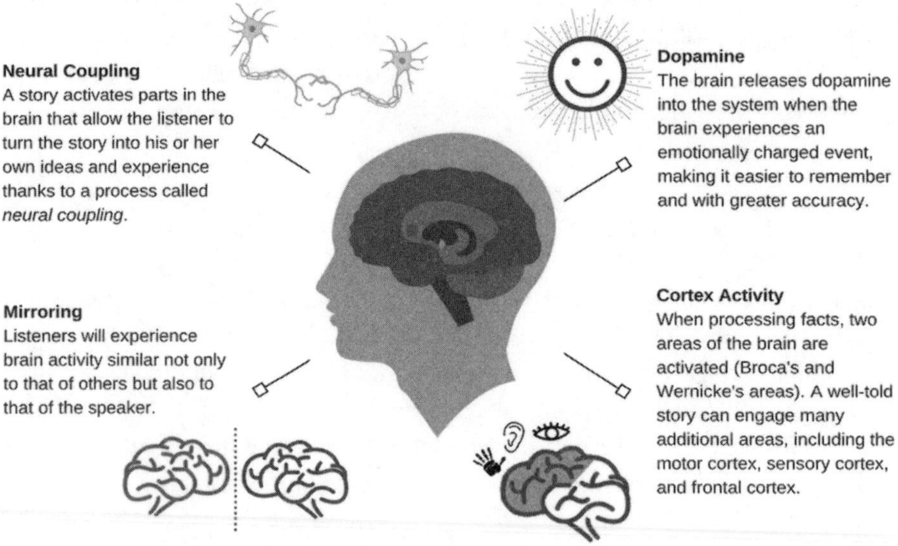

Neural Coupling
A story activates parts in the brain that allow the listener to turn the story into his or her own ideas and experience thanks to a process called *neural coupling*.

Dopamine
The brain releases dopamine into the system when the brain experiences an emotionally charged event, making it easier to remember and with greater accuracy.

Mirroring
Listeners will experience brain activity similar not only to that of others but also to that of the speaker.

Cortex Activity
When processing facts, two areas of the brain are activated (Broca's and Wernicke's areas). A well-told story can engage many additional areas, including the motor cortex, sensory cortex, and frontal cortex.

Figure 5.2 The Impact of an Emotionally Engaging Story

Tool: Neuro Storytelling

Here's the storytelling recipe our clients love to use as they craft their organizational stories.

Step 1. Focus on Your Story Customers and Their Context

Who is the story for? Clients? Prospects? Team members? Take a moment and think about the recipients of the story: what is their context? Notice the situations they are in and make sure they can relate to your stories. Tell stories where they can see themselves as the hero of the piece.

When you tell your story, choose the communication vehicle that fits their context. For example, one client's target customers are parents of small children, and they tell their stories via parenting blogs. Telling the same story on LinkedIn would probably not have been nearly as effective.

Step 2. Make It Authentic

Fabricated stories don't usually have the same emotional impact as real ones. You just can't make up some of those quirky details. As Mark Twain said, "Truth is stranger than fiction."[4] People like stories that have enough specific details to create a picture in their mind. Have a contest and ask your team to submit stories of times when your organization's values were demonstrated. Develop the stories that have the most emotional impact. Remember how emotional engagement affects the brain.

To make it really memorable, it also helps if the story is told by a trusted member of the community. For example, stories told by customers about their own experiences are going to feel more genuine and impactful than ones your company tells about itself.

Step 3. Give the Story Movement

Start your story with a problem or situation, and then show how that problem is resolved. Make sure the story goes from a problem (or a situation that is less than fully desirable) to a more desirable outcome.

The greater the challenge in the story, the more interesting. The more distance between the starting point and the ending point, the more dramatic and compelling. Help us take the journey with you, and we'll share in the triumph.

Step 4. Make It Value Oriented

What value, insight, or service resolved the problem? For example, marketing stories might show how your product or service helped in a unique or challenging situation. Ask yourself: "What desirable outcome happened for the protagonist?"

Make sure your story demonstrates your values. Other stories might be funnier, but you want to promote the ones that communicate your values, who you are, and how you'll show up for others.

Step 5. Test the Efficacy

Try it out. Does the story communicate positively? Test your story on a focus group to make sure it has the intended meaning and impact.

The Internet makes this pretty easy to do, but make sure you have tested your story in a nonrecordable way before you "go big." Stories are memorable, so you want to make sure people are remembering you positively.

Not every story will meet all of the following criteria, but I like to check my clients' stories against the CURVE model from Marketing Profs to make sure their stories are creating a positive experience:

- C is for *curiosity*. Does the recipient want to know what happened?

- U is for *urgency*. Does the story create a sense of "must get this done now!"?

- R is for *relevance*. Is the story relevant to the recipient's situation or context?

- V is for *value*. Does the story reflect my values? Is the story valuable to the recipient?

- E is for *emotion*. Does the story have an emotional impact? Is it funny, scary, surprising, or something else?[5]

Let's go back to the software engineering organization example from the beginning of this chapter. As part of the solution, we helped the interim leader tell a story to connect with the situation all the engineers were facing: losing someone they considered key and valuable. The interim leader addressed the team members (the audience) face-to-face because this was the most appropriate way to communicate with them.

During her talk, the interim leader addressed the team by sharing stories of adversity in her past—when she was overwhelmed by market demands. She told them about how she lost a key engineer and felt deeply discouraged and at a loss as to what to do.

The main message communicated was that her team already had all the skills they needed to succeed, with or without their leader. The key takeaways were that they simply needed a *features team* to vote on which features should be added when to best serve their customers. They could succeed by pulling together. This wasn't the end of the world—just the end of how things had been. And in this new future, they had more power.

With her story, she showed the engineers how to step out of being *victims* and into becoming *outcome creators*. Storytelling helped them release their resistance to the PS and direct their attention to the outcome they wanted to create. *The engineers were empowered to create the conditions they wanted.*

THE POWER OF A STORY WELL TOLD

Remember, stories are potent engagement and teaching tools. They help us navigate change by experiencing it vicariously through the characters in the story. They help us "walk a mile in their moccasins" and "test" the tools the protagonist used. They help us create new beliefs and expand our identity—to see ourselves as bigger, more capable, more powerful than we had previously.

Follow this guide and make sure the stories being told about you and your organization are sending the right message. And then it'll be time to deeply envision and anchor the outcome, the Desired State you want to step into, which we'll cover in the next chapter.

SUMMARY

1. Reframing is a way of viewing and experiencing events, ideas, concepts, and emotions to find more useful alternatives. It helps us change the story we tell ourselves about what is happening or has happened.

2. There are two main types of reframing: context reframing and content reframing. Context reframes work on the principle that every behavior is useful in some context. A difficult or challenging behavior can be reframed in a different context so that it's useful. Content reframes work by changing the actual content of the meaning you gave the behavior, which changes the experience.

3. All leaders need to be great storytellers. People love to tell and hear stories; they are potent engagement and teaching tools. They help us

navigate change by experiencing it vicariously through the characters in the story.

4. Stories we remember have some sort of emotional impact on us. They have this impact because we can relate to the hero and the story line in some way.

5. We connect to the storyteller via mirror neurons; we get deeply engaged and feel, hear, or see and even smell or taste what's happening in the story. The stories you tell about your organization need to be positively impactful in this way too.

TWITTER TAKEAWAYS

- It is not what happens but what it means that matters. Change the meaning, change the feeling.

- Make a game out of shifting the team out of meaning distortions that are pulling you into Critter State.

- Stories are like nutrition for our souls. We remember them and love them. They have deep meaning for us.

- Stories are potent engagement and teaching tools. They help us navigate change by allowing us to experience it vicariously through the characters.

- Stories help us create new beliefs and expand our identity—to see ourselves as bigger, more capable, and more powerful than we had previously.

RESOURCES

See this chapter's section on www.PowerYourTribe.com for the following:

- Chapter *Quick Take* video

- Google's Optimal Teams Research

- Storytelling That Drives Business Results: How to Craft Compelling Stories

- Brand Trust Factor Assessment: How to Assess the Power of Your Brand

CHAPTER 6

Anchor the Outcome You Want

Now that you have choice, what exactly would you like? Once you figure out what you want, you can help others do the same. A clear Desired State combined with potent sensory anchors can make all the difference.

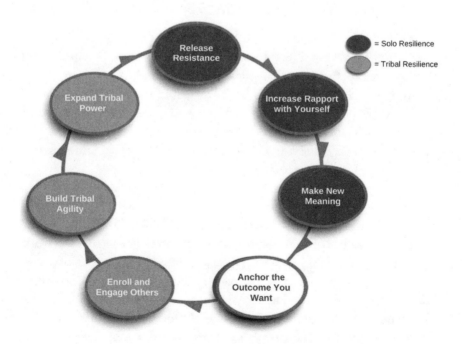

Figure 6.1 The Resilience Cycle: Anchor the Outcome You Want

PROBLEM

Andrew is senior vice president (SVP) of product development at a mid-sized high-tech firm. Because he is the SVP, Andrew's work often involves collaborating with other designers and staff, gaining feedback on his plans and adjusting accordingly. Teamwork is necessary for successful product development.

However, often when Andrew receives feedback on his plan or when the expected result is changed by others in the organization—whether in the form of receiving an e-mail or hearing it in face-to-face discussion—Andrew finds himself getting disappointed. He then spirals down the Emotion Wheel from disappointment to powerlessness and eventually to helplessness. He decides—believes—that his work is not valuable.

Andrew then does what he knows best to manage his experience of helplessness. He gives up, walks outside, and numbs this painful experience with a cigarette.

PROMISE

Do you ever experience this at work? Do you ever find yourself in a downward spiral even when there doesn't seem to be a logical explanation for why you are experiencing what you are experiencing?

When Andrew approached us for coaching, he decided he wanted more choice about the situation, versus reacting negatively when people at his firm changed his product plans. As an experienced professional, Andrew knew that feedback and change were necessary. But knowing that didn't change his *experience* of the situation.

In a coaching session, we unpacked the structure of Andrew's experience first. We identified the triggers (the Vs and As) that were causing the negative feelings (K−). This allowed us to understand how Andrew was creating his experience of hopelessness in response to changes in plans at work.

Then we used *VAK Anchoring* to change the Vs, As, and Ks of his experience of changes to his product plans. When you change the structure, you change the beliefs, and hence you change the experience. We did this to add more choices to Andrew's menu in the form of more positive Ks.

We also used an *Outcome Frame* (introduced in Chapter 3) to clarify exactly what Andrew wanted regarding changes to his plans. Andrew wanted to feel strong and clear on what was needed so he could provide it to others. He wanted to collaborate with them rather than avoiding and walking away from them.

We then used the VAK Anchoring tool again to anchor this new Desired State so that he could step into the more productive behaviors that come with it.

RESULT

By unpacking how Andrew structured his experience, clarifying the outcome he wanted, and anchoring *new* choices, we changed Andrew's experience from disappointment and helplessness to curiosity.

Rather than freezing, walking away, and having a cigarette, Andrew now gets curious (K+) whenever people try to change the plan. He wants to learn more about how they see it and why they have recommended the changes.

Instead of deciding that his work isn't valuable, Andrew feels stronger and clearer about collaborating with his "plan editors" on a solution. He also has a positive feeling of being understood and is proud of his ability to choose his behavior. In short, he is now able to shift from Critter State to Smart State.

•   •   •

When we use the tools of VAK Anchoring and the Outcome Frame to establish new habit patterns, we gain potent new capabilities. These capabilities, or skills, help us choose more empowering and emotionally agile behaviors.

We touched on the Outcome Frame in Chapter 3 when we learned the Maneuvers of Consciousness. In this chapter we'll drill down further into the details so you can clearly understand this powerful tool and how it enables us to first clarify and then create our desired experience (Desired State).

But first, let's make sure that we understand the neurolinguistic structure of human experience and how repetitive and habitual behaviors and responses work.

DRIVING BEHAVIOR CHANGE THAT LASTS USING NEUROSCIENCE

In Part I, we analyzed the structure of human behavior and how it works. Now let's consider the summary formula in Figure 6.2.

**From our environment we receive
visual inputs (Vs) and auditory inputs (As)**
that lead to our

↓

kinesthetic feelings (Ks)
that reinforce or expand or contract our

↓

beliefs and identity
that determine our

↓

capability and behavior,
which then generate a new set of Vs and As, and the cycle repeats.

Figure 6.2 Formula for the Structure of Human Experience

Let's add another layer and consider how our beliefs and our identity actually translate into everyday behavior. We do what we believe we can do based on beliefs about external conditions and internal conditions. Our beliefs about our internal conditions equal our identity. Think of it this way: an external trigger generates an internal positive or negative kinesthetic response (K+ or K−), which generates or reminds us of a belief (often outside of our awareness), which leads to a behavioral routine (the post-trigger behavior sequence to manage the K+ or K−) that results in a reward (a better K). The reward might be simply that a negative feeling stops or decreases (think about reaching for that fifth giant cookie you don't need), or it might be something we really do want (the job is done, and done well). We'll unpack this sequence further in our example with Andrew.

Our beliefs about the world, others, situations, and ourselves drive our behavior. So basically a behavior fires off a new or repeat sequence of Vs and As, which generate Ks, and the process repeats.

VAK ANCHORING: INCREASING OUR BEHAVIOR OPTIONS BY ADDING BETTER CHOICES

We know that people will always, always choose the best feeling available. And if there isn't a good feeling (K+) available, people will choose the behavior with the least bad K. So when people do something that appears to be painful to themselves, it's actually the best option available to them. Other choices with better feelings or more positive beliefs just aren't "on the menu" for the situation they are struggling with.

How do we get better options? How do we expand our menu of choices? Let's take a deeper look at Andrew's example.

Recall that Andrew wanted to respond from choice, versus reacting, when people at his firm changed his product plans. Let's unpack the structure of Andrew's experience first and then use *metacognition* (thinking about thinking) to map out a new behavior choice.

Here's what used to happen.

Old Behavior Pattern (Reaction)

Trigger

Andrew's plan or expected result is changed by others at his organization. In neuro-shorthand this might look something like this:

> External V of seeing e-mail stating changes + internal As of self-talk stating "My work is not valuable" = leads to K– of disappointment

Routine

He feels disappointed, runs more internal Vs (visuals) and As (auditory soundtracks) of his dad asking him to make plans and then constantly changing them, which causes him to feel powerless, which spirals into feeling helpless (more Vs and As outside of his awareness generating more K–s), propelling him into self-talk of "I'm useless"—so he gives up, goes outside to have a cigarette, and numbs the K– (his choice for the best K available). Now no one will get great work from Andrew—he has shut down.

Reward

This behavior reinforces a recurring pattern in Andrew's life, so he is actually invested in continuing it since it has shaped his identity. He knows he can survive it because he has survived many similar experiences. The reward is that he gets to stay safe, withdraw, and not take responsibility for what happens next. Now it's somebody else's decision, not his.

• • •

Routines and rewards don't always feel good, but they do always feel familiar to our creature neurology (our reptilian + mammalian brain combo). That's why we repeat them—they are the best feeling option we have available once the trigger event has occurred.

Internal triggers are hard enough, but when the triggers are outside of us, they feel really out of our control even though we get to choose to respond. The key is learning how to slow down.

New Behavior Pattern (Responding from Choice)

First, Andrew and I needed to create a new routine and a new reward.

The new routine he wanted was to notice that the trigger had occurred and immediately get curious about what other people wanted to achieve with the changes they were suggesting or requesting. He wanted to immediately shift his attention to others and away from the painful meaning he was making that was really an echo of past trauma tied to his dad.

The new reward would be that he'd feel strong, he could respond from choice versus compulsively reacting, and he'd be clear on what was needed so he could provide it to others. He wanted to feel proud that he could choose his behavior in this scenario.

So we recalled times in his life when he had similar positive experiences of behavioral choice. We had him "load up" those memories by recalling their visuals, auditory tracks, and positive kinesthetic feelings (VAK structures). Then we "set an anchor" by having him squeeze his left wrist as he recalled the VAK structures of a specific memory of experiencing a useful emotional state. To make this new routine and reward irresistible, he added multiple similar positive memories one on top of the other ("stacking them up," if you will), so the potency of the anchor increased.

Once he had all of these resources stacked up on his left wrist, he let go of his anchor and jumped up and down a few times to "break" the state he was in. Then I asked him to squeeze his left wrist to test the anchor. It worked—he immediately shifted to a state that included the positive resources we had anchored.

Since human beings are meaning-making machines, if we observe two things happening at the same time, our brains decide they are related, establishing new neural connections. This form of association is how anchoring works. If we create *new* associations (new Vs, As, and Ks), we can change the behavior of a person because we are changing the neural connections in his or her brain. Remember, neurons that fire together wire together.

So here's how Andrew used VAK Anchoring the next time his product plans were changed.

Trigger

Andrew's plan or expected result was changed by others at his organization, and Vs, As, and Ks automatically fired: he saw an e-mail regarding changes or heard someone mentioning changes, and he said to himself, "Oh! Changes coming!"

New Routine

Andrew noticed the trigger and got curious, and he said to himself, "Hmmm . . . let's consider the possibilities here." He used the kinesthetic anchor we set (right hand squeezes left wrist). Now he had a new K and he felt better, so his creature neurology (reptilian + mammalian brain combo) launched the new routine.

With Andrew's new response of curiosity, he sought more information from others. He reached out to the "plan editors" to learn what they would like and why they wanted the changes. (Notice the new Ks, beliefs, and identity that arose here.)

New Reward

Andrew felt strong and clear (more good Ks), and now he had a deeper understanding of what the plan editor wanted so that they could collaborate on a solution. He also had a positive feeling of being understood, and he was proud of his ability to choose his behavior (even more good Ks, as well as positive beliefs and identity).

• • •

So what does this all mean?

We can recall, replicate, and generate experiences for ourselves and others by creating more compelling structures that have better Ks (feelings), and thus we can foster more expansive and positive beliefs and identity.

As leaders, we need to add better Ks to people's menus, whether individually or as a group. Because people will reach for the *most positive* feeling available to them, better choices *will* change their behavior. We can anchor our own optimal or preferred states to increase emotional agility, and we can set anchors to help others as well.

Think about how this might affect your behavior and that of others. What triggers set off routines and rewards in your life? What behaviors would you like to change? How can you use this learning to craft your organization's or product's brand experience? Let's take a deeper look at how VAK Anchoring works so that you can use it yourself.

Tool: VAK Anchoring

We've established that we experience the world through our senses, and we've shown that all key memories as well as emotional experiences have a minimum of a VAK trio associated with them (visual, auditory, and kinesthetic input) and sometimes olfactory and gustatory input too. Anchors call up those sensory states and intentionally "set" a "recall" button in our body.

In other words, as we saw with Andrew's example, we can recall specific reference experiences, associate them with something (*anchor* them to a space, a sound, or a touch), and create the meaning we would like to create.

Let's try it now:

1. **Determine your anchor.** Go ahead and choose it now so that you don't have to interrupt the process below. Pick something unique, something you don't do every day but also something not too unusual because you don't want to call attention to yourself when you fire your anchor. For instance, my "soothing" anchor when I want to relax into sleep at night is to make a very loose fist with my left hand and slide my thumb between my pointer and middle finger. When I "fire" (use) that anchor, it helps me unplug from the day, and I notice I often even say "ahhhhhhh" out loud. Examples for your anchor could be your left hand squeezing your right wrist or

your right pointer finger touching your left elbow. You decide. Make it something easy to fire without others noticing, as well as an area that isn't commonly touched by others so we can regulate when the anchor is fired.

2. **Recall a positive memory with the experience you want.** For example, if you want to create an experience of confidence, recall a memory when you felt confident, when you felt like "I've got this, I know how to do this, I'm 'on' today, here we go!" Step deeply into the memory: see the visuals, hear the sounds, feel the emotional feelings, and notice any aromas or tastes. Look around in the memory and be fully present in it. Feel confidence surging through your cells.

3. **Set your anchor on your body while continuing to recall the memory.** While holding your anchor, increase the positive intensity of the memory, and as soon as it peaks, release your anchor.

Now let's test it. Shake your body out, count backward from 10 to 1 if you need a bit more of a break, and then fire off your anchor again. Did you recall the confident state? If so, awesome! If not, that's OK. Repeat the process, stepping even more deeply into the memory and recalling the VAK trio even more powerfully. Remember what we said in Chapter 3 about how the path of consent and curiosity leads to learning? Get curious and have fun with this!

In time, as you get more comfortable using anchors, you can start helping your family set them. You can help your kids set "homework" anchors (I love this one) or help your spouse set a "love" anchor so they can feel deeply loved and cherished whenever they fire the anchor (or you do). There's nothing like bringing new emotional agility capabilities and behaviors to your tribe both at work and at home.

THE OUTCOME FRAME: DESIGNING THE OUTCOME YOU WANT

A VAK anchor can also be used to anchor a Desired State, which we can create in depth with the Outcome Frame. As we mentioned in Chapter 3, the Outcome Frame can be used with yourself or with others to create a rich, detailed, and compelling Desired State.

I love the Outcome Frame because it's an all-purpose tool to create insights about what people want and how exactly they'll know they received it or achieved it, plus they'll know the cost of getting it (to make sure it's what they truly want—*and* that their system is OK with getting it).

Use it up, down, and across the organizational chart. Use it inside the organization and outside with prospects, clients, and potential partners of any type. Use it to clarify needs, to diffuse or clear conflict, and to help people shift from focusing on the problem at hand to focusing on the outcome they want to create instead.

Some people don't know what they want when they first approach the Outcome Frame. That's OK. In this case, you can warm up by asking yourself what you *don't* want and then asking yourself what the opposite experience would be. If you don't want so much stress, what's the opposite? Do you want more peace, more emotional agility? The following process is a shorter version of the Outcome Frame presented in *SmartTribes*, so if you want to see the Big Daddy of Outcome Frames, you can see it there.[1]

Tool: Outcome Frame

Warm-Up (If Needed)

1. Make a list of three things you don't want, three things that are really making your life a hassle, or even just three things you'd feel better without.

2. Now list the positive alternative to each of the above.

3. Pick the positive alternative you want most.

Excellent. Now answer the following questions.

1. What Would You Like?

To answer this question, be sure to name something you can create and maintain. In other words, answering "For Bob to stop being so annoying" is not a valid outcome. You cannot control Bob. You can, however, control your response to Bob's behavior, and you can cease to be annoyed by it.

So an edit could be "to be peaceful around Bob" or "to be unaffected by Bob's behavior" or "to be peaceful inside, regardless of what is happening at work." Your answer also needs to be a reasonable outcome—something you can achieve in the near future that's not wildly unrealistic.

2. What Will Having That Do for You?

How will you feel when you get this outcome? What will you get? What benefits will you and others receive?

Be sure to ask yourself this question at least three times: "What will having [your answer to question 1] do for me?" and then, based on your answer, ask, "And what will having *that* do for me?" And then, based on *that* answer, ask, "And what will having *that* do for me?" We need to get to the bottom of what the true benefits are.

3. How Will You Know When You Have It?

What criterion or proof will manifest so that you know you actually got it? Make this tangible, measurable, and specific so that you can really step into the Desired State. Shoot for at least three proof points that can be tracked to make sure the outcome was achieved.

4. When, Where, and with Whom Would You Like It?

When specifically would you like the outcome to occur? Where (work or home)? With whom (Bob, or the entire finance team)?

5. What of Value Might You Risk or Lose?

If there were no risk for you to have this outcome, you would have it already. Let's get present to the risk of having it and to what might change if you actually get it. Note that there's often an ego risk. People might fear losing friends if they become more powerful, fear the spotlight of stepping into their power, or fear being less involved in minutia and losing touch with their team.

6. Visualize a Picture Up and to Your Right (Where Your Brain Makes Pictures of the Future) of a Future You That Has the Outcome You Want

In comparison to a kinesthetic anchor, where we use touch, making a picture up and to your right is a *visual anchor*. Can you see that future you? If so, step into that future you. Imagine putting your fingers into your future self's "finger slots," putting your toes into your future self's "toe slots," breathing with your future self's lungs, seeing through your future self's eyes, and hearing with your future self's ears.

Now test having the outcome. What do you see, hear, feel? What's it like having it? Is it worthwhile? Is it helpful? Do you enjoy it? What does your future self believe about yourself? About the situation or organization or world? Note all of this.

If you cannot see a future you with this outcome, think of a person who has the outcome you want and step into that person and test-drive the outcome.

Be sure to bask in this Desired State for at least 15 minutes. You want to make sure it is fully experienced and feels super compelling and worthwhile.

Now anchor this state in your body with a kinesthetic anchor, such as pressing your right thumb into the center of your left palm, if you like. Increase the intensity of the good feelings, and when they peak, release the anchor. You'll want to activate (press) this anchor in the future when you want to recall this state. It'll come in handy as you are moving through your next steps.

7. Your Next Steps

Map out an action plan to start tangibly creating the outcome you want. Make it specific so that when you put this book down, you will be ready to leap into action.

Sample Outcome Frame

Here's a sample Outcome Frame with the answers filled in.

Warm-Up

Make a list of three things you don't want, three things that are really making your life a hassle, or even just three things you'd feel better without:

1. *Too many menial or low-value activities consuming my time*

2. *Annoyed by coworker*

3. *Not enough downtime*

Now list the positive alternative to each of the above:

1. *More time for strategic tasks*

2. *Unaffected by coworker's attitude or behavior*

3. *More relaxation and play time*

1. What Would You Like?

More strategic time

2. What Will Having That Do for You?
I'll feel more engaged and energized, like I'm really making a difference to the business. I'll feel more pride, confidence, peace. I'll feel like I'm doing what I'm supposed to be doing here.

3. How Will You Know When You Have It?
When I spend two hours or more each week on strategy and visioning, when I cut the number of meetings I attend by 25 percent, and when my direct reports are at Leadership Level 5+.[2]

4. When, Where, and with Whom Would You Like It?
Three years ago! Immediately . . . by the middle of the next quarter, it has to be happening.

5. What of Value Might You Risk or Lose?
I may initially feel less important or less involved in minutia. I may have to let go of some control, resist the temptation to rescue, and invest time cultivating directs more powerfully.

6. Visualize a Picture Up and to Your Right (Where Your Brain Makes Pictures of the Future) of a Future You That Has the Outcome You Want
I see a more relaxed me, being far more productive and having more fun at work. My people are more empowered because they are doing more challenging work because I've delegated more of my work to them. Also, since I have more strategic time, I'm a much more effective and lively sounding board for them, and as a result, they're having more compelling and fulfilling insights. This is awesome. I can't wait to create this outcome!

Now anchor this state in your body with a kinesthetic anchor. While holding the anchor, increase the intensity of the good feelings, and when they peak, release the anchor.

7. Your Next Steps

Set up recurring strategic time in my calendar and one-on-ones to delegate some work and build leadership. Determine which meetings to skip and use the "Effective Meetings and Delegation Processes" from the SmartTribes Playbook. (See the Resources section at end of chapter.)

CREATE YOUR DESIRED STATE

Which of your desired outcomes would you like to do an Outcome Frame for? Which will make your life most calm and pleasant now? Pick one from your list and open a new blank document or grab a pen and paper. Step into your Desired State and test the waters.

Now that your desired outcome is clear and anchored, in the next chapter you'll learn more tools to engage intentionally and enroll others to create the outcomes you want together—and increase their emotional agility at the same time.

SUMMARY

1. Experience has structure. Before we change an unwanted experience, we must understand what trigger images or sounds (Vs and As) are creating the Ks, and we need to identify the main decisions and beliefs we have made about those trigger images or sounds.

2. Human beings are meaning-making machines. If two things happen at the same time, our brain decides they are related, establishing new neural connections.

3. VAK Anchoring helps us create new meaning by connecting a new set of Vs, As, and Ks with our experience. When done properly, anchoring will help our brain make new neural connections and add more choices to our behavioral menu.

4. As leaders, we need to add better Ks to people's menus, which will change their behavior because people will reach for the *most positive* feeling available to them.

5. The Outcome Frame helps us create with specificity the Vs, As, and Ks of our Desired State (DS). Once our DS is established, we can imagine what it is like to have what we want and viscerally experience it.

TWITTER TAKEAWAYS

- Our beliefs about the world, others, situations, and ourselves drive our behavior.

- When we see people do something that appears to be painful to themselves, we need to realize that they are doing it only because it's the best option available to them.

- Routines and rewards don't always feel good, but they do always feel familiar to our reptilian + mammalian brain combo. That's why we repeat them.

- What triggers set off routines and rewards in your life? What behaviors would you like to change?

- There's nothing like bringing new emotional agility capabilities and behaviors to your tribe both at work and at home.

RESOURCES

See this chapter's section on www.PowerYourTribe.com for the following:

- Chapter *Quick Take* video

- *Outcome Frame* video

- Communication and Meeting Types: Unpack and Optimize How Your Team Communicates

- Effective Meeting Process: How to Reduce Meetings and Meeting Time by up to 50 Percent

- Effective Delegation Process: How to Get "One and Done"

CHAPTER 7

Enroll and Engage Others

Forge your emotional agility strategy with others: enroll, align, and engage even the most challenging types to help you create the needed change.

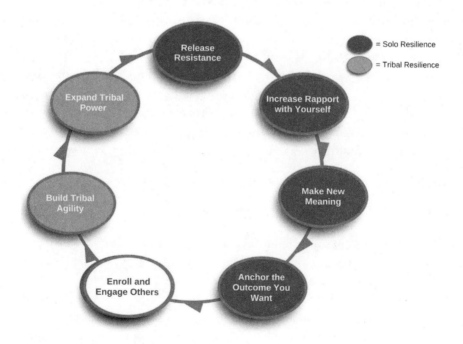

Figure 7.1 The Resilience Cycle: Enroll and Engage Others

PROBLEM

A midsized financial services organization had a challenge: the leadership team was deeply disconnected. This was because the CEO had an inner circle whose members had special privileges yet didn't perform to agreed-upon targets, whereas the "other" leaders scrambled to accommodate the CEO's "strategy of the second" (which often changed day to day). Since the strategy changes were disclosed in advance only to his inner circle, the other leaders had to quickly pivot, which confused and frustrated their teams—and resulted in tons of wasted time. The only people with visibility were the CEO and his inner circle. Everyone else was in the dark.

The team members as well as the "other" leaders were constantly on high alert. They lived in firefighting mode, and they were dealing with constantly changing plans—the CEO's strategies were revealed to the "outside" group in only small fragments, and with great urgency.

Many team members were running around like their hair was on fire, arms in the air, while shaking their heads and murmuring, "I don't believe this! Again?" Others were just in shock and disbelief: "Whoa! We're doing that? I never knew that! I wouldn't have spent $X on such and such if I had known we were going to be shifting our focus away."

The result was high distrust between the "in" and "out" groups. And since so many fires had to be put out regularly, the team wasn't focused on what they should've been: key performance indicators. Operational efficiency and effectiveness were at an all-time low, key players were job hunting, profitability was plunging, and a lot of redundant work was being done.

PROMISE

Does that problem sound familiar? Have you had disconnected team members in key roles as a result of poor communication? Have you had "special ones" who were in the loop while everyone else was scrambling to understand the organization's goals?

When situations like this arise, it's key to stop, take a temperature check, find out where the infection is, and get some good medicine to the patient to bring about a rapid recovery.

And that's what we did. A Safety, Belonging, and Mattering (SBM) Index was just what the doctor ordered. The *SBM Index* is a swift and effective diagnostic tool to gauge employee engagement and diagnose cultural disconnects. First, we had to find out exactly where the trouble was at the departmental level and then exactly what the key issues were. Once we were clear on the cures needed, we helped the client put key cultural programs in place while we taught all the leaders *Meta Programs* so that they could communicate in the language of a given recipient. This would help the communication "land"—that is, it would help the communication be received swiftly and accurately—because the leader was speaking in the communication recipient's "language." In addition, we coached the CEO on *SBM Communication*, expanding the "in" group to include all those who needed to be involved and, of course, holding everyone to the same performance standard to foster a culture of fairness.

RESULT

Fast-forward six months: the CEO was no longer playing favorites, the leaders were all aligned, and their direct reports understood what the goals were and how to achieve them. Now they knew who was craving what (safety, belonging, and/or mattering), how to give it to them, and how to boost performance and engagement.

As you know very well by now, whenever you're in a growth or change scenario, chances are your team will be in Critter State sometimes. Often, as leaders, you are focusing so intensely on growth that you can miss that your team's emotional experience is suffering. The SBM Index is a fantastic way to find out what people are feeling and keep your finger on the pulse of each department and the organization overall, and the Meta Programs can then help you communicate in a way that connects.

SAFETY, BELONGING, AND MATTERING: GIVE YOUR TRIBE WHAT THEY CRAVE

As we discussed in Chapter 2, to become resilient and shift to our Smart State, we must have safety, belonging, and mattering. But how do you know who needs what and when? We use three main tools to find out: (1) the

SBM Behavior Decoder and (2) the corresponding SBM Communication tools for individuals and (3) the SBM Index for the entire organization.

Tool: SBM Behavior Decoder

Very often you don't even have to ask if a team member needs safety, belonging, or mattering. His or her behavior says it all. Table 7.1 is an SBM Behavior Decoder that might help you give them what they need to shift to their Smart State.

TABLE 7.1 SBM Behavior Decoder

Behavioral Clues	What They Might Crave	How You Can Help
Gossip, rumors, spreading fear via talking about disaster, pain, or hurt, talking about contingency plans, planning their exit, fighting back, or saying they are frozen or can't move forward	Safety	Talk with them about their concerns, form contingency plans, discuss dependencies required in order to get what they want, and normalize their experience as something that happens during growth and change. Assure them that you have their back and that you're in this together.
Isolating, withholding information, dropping out of contact or not replying to e-mails, text messages, or voice mail, forming silos, talking about how they're on their own	Belonging	Tell them how happy you are that they're on the team, ask for their ideas on increasing communication and information sharing, and involve them in a team project.
Condescension, arrogance, shutting others down, being overly self-focused, talking about how they aren't valued or appreciated	Mattering	Call out their key strengths, and have them lead a key initiative.

If people are in their Critter State and craving safety, they'll take safety away from others. They need their outside world to match their inside world. This could manifest in the workplace as someone spreading gossip, rumors, or fear in general.

If people are in their Critter State and craving belonging, they'll isolate, withhold information, or form silos—they will essentially "leave the tribe." They feel they don't belong, so they'll make sure that they don't behave accordingly, so the outside world reflects their inside experience.

If people are in their Critter State and craving mattering, they'll take mattering away from others via condescending behavior and making people feel small. They don't matter, so they make sure that others don't either. Then the world will make sense.

When we give people what they crave, their critter brain calms down, and we can guide them into their Smart State. This is where true rapport, connection, alignment, enrollment, and engagement live. Oh—and high performance, collaboration, and sustainability are the results! Remember, safety + belonging + mattering = trust.

Tool: SBM Communication

Once we identify what others need (safety, belonging, and/or mattering), we can provide it remarkably quickly with the right words.

Giving Others What They Crave

Let's say people are craving safety. You know this because they often talk about not feeling safe, and when they are in their Critter State, they take safety away (misery loves company) and instill fear in others. Here's some wording that validates their feelings and could even talk them "off the ledge": "You are doing everything correctly. Thanks for stretching! I've got your back. Reach out to me if I can provide any clarity, brainstorming, or support of any kind." With communication like that, the critter brain (our fight/flight/freeze/faint response) says, "Ahhhhhh." Now the risk-averse or fearful people can rise up, take more risks, innovate better, and collaborate better. You're helping them shift into their Smart State and feel safe.

What if people crave belonging and want to feel like they are part of a group and know they have equal value? First, look at how they act in the Critter State—most likely, they are isolating themselves and/or forming silos and divisions within the larger group. Here's some belonging messaging: "I'm so glad you're on the team. It's great to have you here. Who could you bring into the loop or mentor to help them succeed too and to expand our tribe?" You're giving them the experience of belonging and helping them spread it to others.

If people crave mattering, they want to feel appreciated, and they want to feel like they are making a difference. When they are in their Critter State, they take mattering away—they make people feel small and invisible and/or unimportant. Here's some messaging: "You're my top pick to run this project. I totally trust and appreciate you and your contributions and gifts. How can I help you shine?" You're showing them they matter and that you appreciate their talents.

How to Ask Someone to Give You What You Crave

Now, rather than focusing on giving others what they crave, what if you want to clearly communicate what you're craving? Here are three examples of how you can do that:

Safety: "I want to be the best [executive/leader/partner] I can be. Could you help me create structures, techniques, or processes to foster innovation, encourage safe and sane risk taking, and meet intellectual challenges? I think this could really help us grow and stretch."

Belonging: "I want to be the best [executive/leader/partner] I can be. Could you brainstorm some ideas with me to create opportunities to bring people together, to form teams, and help them perform at their peak? I would love to contribute in this way."

Mattering: "I want to be the best [executive/leader/partner] I can be. Could you let me know when you're happy with my [work/contributions] and what specifically you like? This will help me do more of what matters to you and the organization."

Every employee, every family member, can be happier and more effective if you simply identify which of these three needs are programmed into their subconscious so powerfully that they literally crave them. Which do you crave? Which do the most important people in your life crave?

Influencing Phrases

Here are four *Influencing Phrases* that are especially helpful when people are in their Critter State and we want to help them feel safe enough to shift out of it:

1. **"What if...?"** When you use this preface to an idea or suggestion, you remove ego and reduce emotion. You're curious—not forcing

a position but rather, scratching your head and pondering. This enables people to brainstorm more easily with you.

2. **"I need your help with . . . ."** We call this a *dom-sub swap* because when the dominant people use it, they are enrolling the subordinate people and asking them to rise up and swap roles. This is an especially effective phrase when you want people to change their behavior or take on more responsibility.

3. **"Would it be helpful if . . . ?"** When people are stuck in their Critter State and spinning or unable to move forward, offering a solution will help them see a possible course of action or positive outcome. This question requires them to assess whether your suggestion is indeed helpful or not—which engages their prefrontal cortex and shifts them into their Smart State.

4. **"Can you help me understand . . . ?"** Sometimes we don't understand the logic path or pitch people are making or even what it is that they want. This phrase helps us gain clarity with a humble, nonconfrontational request. Heck, we could be totally missing their point, so it is best to seek clarity without making any judgments.

Do you see how all four reinforce safety, belonging, and mattering?

Tool: SBM Index

Now that you can more easily recognize and provide SBM to individuals, what is the SBM level of your tribe as a whole? Let's find out with the SBM Index.

The SBM Index is a survey asking respondents how much they agree with 10 statements: 3 on safety, 3 on belonging, 3 on mattering, plus an additional Net Promoter Score (NPS)-like question—because it's really helpful to know if your tribe would recommend working at your organization to their friends. Additional comments are always helpful too.

SBM Index Survey Questions

Following the scale below are our recommended statements for the SBM Index. Consider which ones work best for your culture and feel free to edit them as you see fit—just keep them in groups of safety, belonging, and mattering to extract the benefit of this tool.

Each answer is equivalent to a certain number of points. The highest possible number of points for a given question is 10. It's much easier to have an employee engagement score that is numerical and on a scale of 0 to 100 because people can readily translate those scores into A, B, or C grades, which they can then easily understand and work with. Here is a sample scale for each question in the SBM Index:

Never = 0

Rarely = 2.5

Somewhat consistently = 5

Consistently = 7.5

Always = 10

And here are the SBM Index statements:

1. It's safe to try new approaches, to innovate, to be vulnerable, and to share my ideas at work.

   Comments:

2. When I make a mistake, I am corrected with respect and the desire to help me improve.

   Comments:

3. I have the tools and resources necessary to perform my work to my best ability.

   Comments:

4. I understand the expectations of me and my performance.

   Comments:

5. I trust my team members and colleagues to support my success and the organization's success.

   Comments:

6. I am motivated by and find meaning in the organization's mission, vision, and values.

   Comments:

7. I receive acknowledgment and appreciation at work.

   Comments:

8. I have a career development path that the organization supports me in.

   Comments:

9. I feel I matter to the organization—I am making a difference here.

   Comments:

10. Would you refer your friends to work at [organization]?

    Comments:

Be sure to have a comments section for each statement. It's where some of the biggest nuggets of gold will show up—and the harshest feedback. That's OK because you need to know this. Beware of *survey fatigue* too, which dilutes results. We recommend that surveys have a maximum of 10 items and that the surveys be given at well-spaced intervals so that people don't feel that they are being asked to complete them too often.

Also, be sure to send an SBM-rich e-mail when asking people to take the SBM Index survey, and send another e-mail afterward to thank them, to share what you learned from the survey and what you intend to change.

Presenting the Results

Once you get the results, it's essential to present the SBM Index data in a format the leadership team can easily understand. We recommend a heat map approach. A *heat map* presents the numbers with color coding so that it's very clear where leaders need to focus and where everything is OK.

Table 7.2 is an example from the first SBM Index we did (although in the table we have used different scales of gray rather than color coding) with the financial services organization I mentioned at the beginning of the chapter.

TABLE 7.2 An Example of an SBM Index Report

	Administration	Investments	Marketing	Operations	Sales	Entire Company
Completed Surveys	60%	57%	79%	61%	70%	77%
Q1: It's safe to try new approaches, to innovate, to be vulnerable, and to share my ideas at work.	7.39	4.12	7.73	6.72	6.38	6.44
Q2: When I make a mistake, I am corrected with respect and the desire to help me improve.	6.52	4.85	7.73	6.09	7.00	6.38
Q3: I have the tools and resources necessary to perform my work to my best ability.	7.17	5.44	7.95	6.41	7.25	6.81
Total Safety Satisfaction	70%	48%	78%	64%	69%	65%
Q4: I understand the expectations of me and my performance.	5.33	3.82	6.14	4.84	6.25	5.26
Q5: I trust my team members and colleagues to support the success of the company and me.	5.54	3.53	6.45	4.69	5.88	5.06
Q6: I am motivated by and find meaning in the company's mission, vision, and values.	4.78	3.38	5.00	5.00	6.13	4.89
Total Belonging Satisfaction	52%	36%	59%	48%	61%	50%
Q7: I receive acknowledgment and appreciation at work.	4.46	2.06	3.18	4.84	3.88	3.76
Q8: I have a career development path that the company supports me in.	6.63	5.15	6.82	7.03	7.00	6.52

	Administration	Investments	Marketing	Operations	Sales	Entire Company
Q9: I feel I matter to the company. I am making a difference here.	8.04	7.94	7.73	8.28	7.75	7.96
Total Mattering Satisfaction	64%	51%	59%	67%	62%	61%
Q10: Would you refer your friends to work at your organization?	7.07	7.06	5.68	7.66	7.63	7.13
Overall Satisfaction	62.9%	47.0%	64.4%	64.6%	65.2%	60.2%

Would we have had a more accurate read on the state of the organization if we had incorporated more department-level, as opposed to company-wide, survey participation? Absolutely. But this was the best we could get, so we got to work. In Chapter 8 you'll see the initial programs we put in place. Once the programs were generating results, we achieved greater survey uptake on our next round because people felt safe to provide feedback.

In presenting your results, we suggest sorting all the comments per department. You'll be able to do this because you'll have a unique survey link for each department. Be sure to see the SBM Index resource for this chapter—it'll help you implement yours optimally.

Most of our clients send out an SBM Index questionnaire every six to nine months. In the interim, they launch programs to address the top issues from the prior SBM Index. Make sure you have enough time to create the programs and have them in place for a while so that you will be able to see improvement before you launch your next SBM Index.

Once you complete your own SBM Index, you'll be able to apply the tools and programs described in Chapter 8 to increase your tribe's SBM Index scores.

META PROGRAMS: HOW TO INFLUENCE ANYONE, ANYTIME, ANYWHERE

Even though using words to communicate SBM to your tribe is a great start, if you truly want to enroll and engage your tribe in creating the outcomes you want, you need to go deeper than words.

How many times have you tried to influence, enroll, or engage someone in the past two weeks? How many times were you successful?

People misunderstand one another daily. Why? Because we are speaking different languages—and I'm not talking about Spanish and English or another combo. We're speaking different languages at a subterranean, subconscious, primal level. Everyone deletes, distorts, and generalizes information about the environment differently. Therefore, every human being has his or her own unique map of the world. His or her map is created based on the environment in which he or she was raised and many other factors (Figure 7.2). As a result, we are all, essentially, speaking different languages. And this is how misunderstandings occur.

Figure 7.2 The Influences on Each Individual's Unique Map of the World

Leaders need to be able to influence outcomes. Good intentions are rarely assumed, people are on the lookout for manipulative tactics, and even subtle persuasion efforts are suspect. Real influence is about forging deep connections quickly, stepping into someone's world authentically, and striving for consistent win-win outcomes. It means creating an experience of "same as."

Safe = "Same As"

As human beings, we all need to feel that others are similar to ("same as") us in order to feel we belong together and can move forward together.[1]

Consider the origin of the potent words *belong* and *include*.

The origin and etymology of *belong* are from the Middle English *belongen: be* (make, create) + *longen* (suitable).

When we belong, we are "deemed suitable," which supports our sense of mattering. We are worthy. When we belong, we are also safe. We are not alone. We are included.

The origin and etymology of *include* are from the Old English *in + claudere* (enclose, close in).

When we include people, we enclose them. We bring them toward us.

We are always scanning our world to see if we belong. Did we get invited to something? Did we get a good table at the restaurant? Are my colleagues at the water fountain talking about me?

The rules of belonging are often implicit—and often change. This is one reason why powerful, consistently honored, and frequently communicated mission, vision, and values are so key—they help us understand how we belong in the tribe. (We'll talk more about this in Chapter 8.) Again, if we belong, we are safe—and we matter.

To deeply influence, enroll, and engage our tribe, we need to help tribe members feel that they belong, that they have the experience of "same as." But how do we accomplish that if we don't even speak the same language—even when we think we do? That's where Meta Programs come in.

Tool: Meta Programs

Meta Programs are one of the most potent neuroscience techniques we teach because they enable us to most deeply see someone else's map of the world. Meta Programs were discovered by Leslie Cameron-Bandler in the 1980s and expanded by Rodger Bailey.[2] The advertising industry has been using them ever since.

Meta Programs are the filters through which we see the world—that is, the ways our brains process the world and determine how we react to it. When we speak to people using their Meta Programs, they not only hear what we're saying but they also feel they belong with us, that we are the "same as" they are.

When you understand people's Meta Programs, you understand how they experience the world, what motivates them, how their identity is structured, and what some of their beliefs are. It's work learning them, but it's well worth it if you want deeper rapport with others and deeper connection and fulfillment in your human interactions. Meta Programs enable you to take safety, belonging, and mattering to a whole new level. If personality tests are equivalent to the third floor of a building, Meta Programs are the subbasement. These are deep, embedded "programs" of who you are and how you interact with the world, information, and decisions. Meta Programs support the structure of a person's identity and belief system, which is far deeper than his or her personality.

Because Meta Programs allow you to gain access to a person's emotional brain and establish deep subconscious rapport, they can be powerfully persuasive. That's why we use Meta Programs only for good and not evil. We use them to understand, enroll, engage, and align—not to control, dominate, or manipulate. It's all about intention. What is your intention when you communicate with someone?

The Six Primary Meta Programs

There are many Meta Programs—about 60—according to Leslie Cameron-Bandler, and if you want a super deep dive into Meta Programs, check out Shelle Rose Charvet's book *Words That Change Minds*. Think of each Meta Program as a color and each person as a unique artwork formed by the combination of those colors. Here are the six Meta Programs our clients find most impactful:

1. **Direction: Toward-Away.** Are you motivated to go toward a goal or away from pain? Think salesperson versus accountant: what criteria do they assess situations with?

2. **Reason: Options-Procedures.** Do you like to have many options and choices, or do you prefer a proven step-by-step process? What feels right to you?

3. **Scope: General-Specific.** Do you feel comfortable with a high-level overview, or do you want specific details? When describing something, do you start with the details or the summary?

4. **Orientation: Active-Reflective.** Do you use short sentence structures and high action, or do you want to think about things first, using longer sentence structures with many clauses?

5. **Source: Internal-External.** How do you know you've done a good job? Through external feedback or internal monitoring?

6. **Motivation: Sameness-Difference.** What's your tolerance for change? Do you like things to stay the same, to stay the same but with the hassles removed and more good stuff added, or to change really often or completely?

Just like safety, belonging, and mattering, Meta Programs are contextual, meaning that you may have one set of Meta Programs in the context of work, another set when it comes to money, and yet another for romantic love—although we generally have a set for how we approach life overall. Meta Programs also operate on a range: we don't usually fall all the way to one extreme or the other.

Meta Programs are equally useful whether the person you're addressing is a team member, a board member, a sales prospect, a client, your mother-in-law, your teenager, or the recipient of a marketing message. Speaking to people using their Meta Programs ensures profound rapport, builds connection and trust, and leads to outcomes that are better for everyone.

With regard to Meta Programs, we can ask people specific questions, observe their responses, and elicit their specific Meta Programming to determine *how* those people will behave in life and business.

Now let's look at each category in more detail so that you can begin to decode the Meta Programs of those in your own tribe. For more details about each of these Meta Programs, as well as two more Meta Programs that are essential in sales and marketing scenarios, see www.PowerYour Tribe.com.

Direction: Toward-Away

Here's the approximate distribution of this Meta Program in the U.S. workforce:

Toward	Equal Toward-Away	Away
←		→
40 percent	20 percent	40 percent

Decoder Question: To find out whether people are Toward or Away, ask, "What do you want in your work [or something else important to them]?" (Table 7.3). Keep asking questions such as "What else do you want?" or "What else is important?" Notice what descriptor words they use. Do they want to achieve or attain, or do they want to prevent disaster or solve problems, or do they want to hold down the fort? Be sure to keep a written running score so that your own Meta Programs don't filter what you hear. If you have an extreme bias, you may hear one mention of the other pole as extreme when actually the person is middle-of-the-road.

TABLE 7.3 Toward-Away Meta Program Table

	Toward	Away
Description and motivations	Motivated to achieve goals; to move forward; get what they want.	Motivated to solve problems and mitigate risk, prevent pain.
Advantages	Have lots of energy and momentum; inspire others to action; provide a compelling vision for others to latch on to.	Are the "voice of reason," grounded, and realistic. They appreciate and understand the risks and what problems may occur.
Disadvantages	Toward people can be so goal oriented that they don't focus on, appreciate, or accept what is needed to make goals happen—all the work others will have to do that takes time. Toward people are often impatient; they will already be focused on the next goal, so they may not appreciate the achievement of the current goal.	Away people can be too cautious, and they may appear resistant to take action. Sometimes they are seen as negative or "downers" rather than as a solid sounding board.
Influential words	"Get," "attain," "achieve," and synonyms of these.	"Avoid," "prevent," "assess," "consider," and synonyms of these.
Often found in	CEOs, sales, business development, software development, and design.	Accounting, operations, risk management, nonlitigation legal roles.
Possible conflicts	The Toward person may discount the Away person's point of view, may think he's dragging his feet or just doesn't "get it." The Away person may feel the Toward person is all about the vision, when what really matters is its execution and risks. Disrespect on both sides can cause tremendous tension.	

Reason: Options-Procedures

Here's the approximate distribution of this Meta Program in the U.S. workforce:

Options   Equal Options-Procedures   Procedures

←——————————————————————————————————————→

40 percent   20 percent   40 percent

Decoder Question: To find out whether a person is Options or Procedures, ask, "Why did you choose your current [work/job/car]?" (Table 7.4). An Options person will respond with her criteria or a list of features or traits—for example, for a car: "It gets great gas mileage, it's black, and it's fast." A Procedures person will respond with a story that details a process through which the car was the end point: "Well, you know, it's a funny thing. My old car was breaking down all the time, and my aunt Sue was visiting, and . . . ," and then a story will unfold with a series of steps leading ultimately to the purchase of the car.

TABLE 7.4 Options-Procedures Meta Program Table

	Options	Procedures
Description and motivation	Motivated by choice, possibility, and variety; will give you a list of criteria they want.	Motivated by following a proven and reliable process; will lay out a step-by-step process, or they will need one provided for them.
Advantages	See many ways to solve problems, to implement ideas, and to make things happen. The world is their oyster.	Very reliable and consistent in delivering results by following specific procedures. You can count on them not to cut corners and to follow the rules.
Disadvantages	Options people can create so many choices that they get stuck and don't act, or they present so many options to their team that their strategy and priorities become unclear — again slowing results.	Procedures people can often suffer from rigid thinking and tunnel vision. They are stressed out when a clear procedure isn't provided or when procedures across the organization are inconsistent or differ for similar tasks.

	Options	**Procedures**
Influential words	"Variety," "choice," "possibility," and synonyms of these.	"The right way," "series of steps," "reliable process," and synonyms of these.
Often found in	All roles, though they often gravitate toward anything with "design," "development," or similar words in the title that indicate there is room to operate differently. Options people love to create processes for *other* people to follow.	All roles, though they often gravitate toward accounting, manufacturing, legal, engineering, and other process-driven fields.
Possible conflicts	When an Options person presents too many choices, a Procedures person may shut down or feel so overwhelmed that he won't know how to proceed. When a Procedures person tries to force a process on an Options person, conflict will arise. A better approach is to "interview" the Options person to determine the procedures she needs.	

Scope: General-Specific

Here's the approximate distribution of this Meta Program in the U.S. workforce:

General   Equal General-Specific   Specific

←——→

60 percent   25 percent   15 percent

Decoder Question: To find out whether people are General or Specific, ask questions like "How do you brainstorm challenges at work?" or "How do you solve problems?" or "Describe your weekend" or "What do you do for fun?" (Table 7.5). Notice which influential words they use and notice if they start with specific details or with an overall summary statement.

TABLE 7.5 General-Specific Meta Program Table

	General	Specific
Description and motivations	Motivated to summarize and think at a high level. Looking at the forest.	Motivated by details and sequences. Know how many trees the forest contains, how many leaves each tree has, and the variation of their barks.
Advantages	Have a broad perspective and can see the net-net, they don't get caught up in the details, and they keep momentum moving.	Catch the crucial details that, if overlooked, could be problematic. Provide thorough execution and can answer questions with the key components to ensure that decision-making is accurate.
Disadvantages	General people can stay at too high a level and fail to execute or fail to help others execute, and they may be perceived as glib or vague. They may also make decisions while lacking crucial data.	Can get lost in the details and can lose sight of the goal, the overall strategy, the priorities, and the results.
Influential words	"Overview," "the big picture," "in general," "the point is," and synonyms of these. Start with setting up the frame or context.	"Specifically," "exactly," "precisely," and synonyms of these. Start at detail level and build to conclusion.
Often found in	CEO and all leadership roles; market and strategy development roles.	Engineering, legal, accounting, operations, and market research roles.
Possible conflicts	A General person may gloss over details or not take the time to drill down on them, dismissing the Specific person for being too nitpicky or for bringing up information that seems (to the General person) irrelevant. The Specific person may see the General person as not committed, unrealistic, or irresponsible.	

Orientation: Active-Reflective

Here's the approximate distribution of this Meta Program in the U.S. workforce:

Active	Equal Active-Reflective	Reflective
←		→
15 to 20 percent	60 to 65 percent	15 to 20 percent

Decoder Question: To find out whether people are Active or Reflective, ask questions such as "How do you discover opportunities or challenges?" or "When do you know when your attention is needed?" or "How do you learn new things?" (Table 7.6). Listen for action versus analysis.

TABLE 7.6 Active-Reflective Meta Program Table

	Active	**Reflective**
Description and motivations	Motivated to take action immediately and to charge ahead.	Motivated to analyze, ponder, think through carefully, wait, and react when appropriate.
Advantages	Can be counted on to take the initiative, rally the troops, and go-go-go. They value getting it done yesterday, no matter the cost.	Carefully assess input before taking action. They value getting it right over getting it done.
Disadvantages	Active people can be too hasty in their forward momentum, not considering the risks involved. They can also be so impatient to act that they leave out key people or go against the optimal order of tasks or projects.	Reflective people can be perfectionistic, get stuck in analysis paralysis, or be too slow to take action. They can be seen as less valuable or as not having leadership potential—which is untrue.
Influential words	"Get it done," "now," "don't wait," and synonyms of these.	"Consider," "could," "understand," "think about," and synonyms of these.
Often found in	Sales and other customer-facing and initiating roles.	Research, analysis, customer service, and service.
Possible conflicts	There is high potential for the Active person to dismiss the Reflective person as a passive order taker. This is far from the truth. The Reflective person can see the Active person as acting for the sake of action and not thinking her actions through. Active people benefit from slowing down and considering more; reflective people benefit from having clear and firm final deadlines.	

Source: Internal-External

Here's the approximate distribution of this Meta Program in the U.S. workforce:

Internal	Equal Internal-External	External

←——————————————————————————————————————→

40 percent	20 percent	40 percent

Decoder Question: To find out whether people are Internal or External, ask, "How do you know you've done a good job?" (Table 7.7). Internal people will know because of something—often a feeling—inside themselves. Answers will often be something like "I just know." External people will refer to other people's opinions, quotes, or testimonials, facts and figures, recent promotions, or other forms of public recognition.

TABLE 7.7 Internal-External Meta Program Table

	Internal	External
Description and motivations	Motivated to decide on their own internal standards — don't expect them to seek or respond to external praise and incentives.	Motivated by external praise and rewards.
Advantages	Are generally very self-directed and "low maintenance."	It's easy to incentivize them with bonuses, prizes, and recognition. It's very clear where they stand.
Disadvantages	Internal people can be tough to manage and incentivize, and there will be problems if their internal bar of excellence or accomplishment is out of sync with their manager's.	External people can be too dependent on outside praise or attention, and they may be perceived as draining and needy or as working only for the prize and not for the mission.
Influential words	"What do you think," "it's up to you," and synonyms of these. This is where giving special challenges or cool projects can be effective versus public recognition and rewards (which they don't care about — they already know they're great at their job).	"Others will notice," "feedback you'll get," "raise your profile," "award," "acknowledge," and synonyms of these.

	Internal	External
Often found in	Engineering, manufacturing, legal, and leadership roles.	Sales, marketing, and other outward-facing roles.
Possible conflicts	An Internal person may disregard or even mock organization incentives and cultural rituals of recognition if she feels the culture is too concerned with them (and key accountability structures aren't in place). An External person can become too dependent on prizes or praise, and he may lose motivation if constant incentives aren't offered.	

Motivation: Sameness-Difference

This Meta Program has a wide range, from Sameness through Difference with identifiable sorts in between. It is essentially about how people tolerate change.

Sameness people like change about every 25 years. Difference people will prompt change every six months to 2 years. In this case change does not mean the Difference people leave, but they do have to recommit.

In the middle of this range is Sameness with Exception, which is where most American workers fall (change every five to seven years: the famous "seven-year itch"). This Meta Program has some change tolerance as long as it makes sense—for example, they are fine with Coca-Cola Zero because it is good old Coke with the calories removed. If consistency is provided and extra good things are added or annoying things are removed, the Sameness with Exception people will thrive. This is why we coach leaders to use the words *growth, progress,* and *evolution* as opposed to *change.* Change can hurl us into our critter brain, whereas growth messaging puts us in our prefrontal cortex, where we want to solve puzzles, have visions, and be creative.

The most unusual iteration is Sameness with Exception and Difference. These people want some consistency with the occasional revolution—a rare combo. On average they like change every three to five years, with five to seven years in some contexts and up to two years in others.

Here's the approximate distribution of this Meta Program in the U.S. workforce:

Same	Same with Exception	Same with Exception + Difference	Difference
5 percent	65 percent	10 percent	20 percent

Decoder Question: To find out where a person is on the range of Sameness to Difference, ask (and the wording in this one is very important), "What is the relationship between your work this year and last year?" (Table 7.8). Most people will look at you blankly and ask you to explain the question. Don't explain it. Just ask them to answer as best they can, and repeat the question verbatim. Sameness people will look for all the things that are the same even if they moved from accounting to sales, changed companies, and physically moved to a different state. "Well, I'm still working with numbers and doing calculations." Difference people will tell you everything is completely different even if the only change was to move to the next cubicle: "Oh, my gosh, it's a completely different view!"

TABLE 7.8 Sameness-Difference Meta Program Table

	Sameness	**Difference**
Description and motivations	Motivated by what's in common and by preventing change.	Motivated by radical, total, and/or revolutionary change.
Advantages	Maintaining the status quo can be helpful if the changes haven't been well thought out or don't have a clear and compelling communication strategy. You can count on them; you know where you stand and what they'll be doing for a long time.	Innovation and evolution are key in several fields. The people driving a state of dissatisfaction with the status quo can be key leaders and bring tremendous energy to innovation.
Disadvantages	Sameness people can be excessively fearful and rigidly resistant to change — which is often simply growth.	Difference people can be so pro-change that they break things simply to provide the buzz of changing them, usually at unnecessary expense and time spent. Sometimes it's hard to know what they stand for.
Influential words	"Consistent," "same," "stable," and synonyms of these.	"Disruptive," "change," "different," "revolution," and synonyms of these.
Often found in	Roles with high stability and routine.	Leading-edge research and development roles across technology and other fields.
Possible conflicts	These two roles can clash when management is in one Meta Program and staff is in the other. This is a fairly rare scenario, however.	

As I mentioned, safety, belonging, and mattering Meta Programs are contextual. Table 7.9 illustrates this concept. *Note:* The "SBM Trigger" refers to simply what people crave most: safety, belonging, mattering, or a combination.

TABLE 7.9 Safety, Belonging, and Mattering and Meta Programs in Context

Sample Context	SBM Trigger	Meta Programs
Leading your organization and focused on growth and cultivation.	Mattering: "Let's make a dent in the universe! Let's change the world!"	Toward: "Let's grow!" Options: "Wow, there are so many possibilities!" General: "Let's own the market!" Active: "Let's try it. If it doesn't work, we'll do something else."
Leading your team and dealing with "people issues" that make you uncomfortable.	Safety and belonging: "Let's figure out how to work together so we can rely on one another (and reduce drama)."	Away: "Solve problems before conflict occurs." Procedures: "What's the process to give feedback and create an improvement plan or terminate someone?" Specific: "How, exactly? I don't want to get sued." Reflective: "I want to make sure this is the right thing to do, and I want to do it right."
Parenting: Assume this is your first child and he or she is an infant.	Safety: "OMG, I am responsible for a human life. I don't want to mess it up!"	Away: "Don't hurt the baby!" Procedures: "What's the proven process for taking care of a kid and keeping the kid safe and healthy? What do I need to do next?" Specific: "What exactly am I supposed to do here?" Reflective: "I keep reading and researching and thinking about the baby—I'll take action when I'm sure of what to do."

Sample Context	SBM Trigger	Meta Programs
Parenting: Now the first child is a tween or teen and is somewhat independent, and you've established that you know how to parent — and the child has made it this far.	Belonging: "Let's hang out!"	Toward: "Sure, go out for football!" Options: "What are all the cool things we can do together?" General: "We'll figure this out." Active: "Let's do it!"

How do we use Meta Programs? They're best used at turning points, such as when we are working on the following:

- Recruiting or interviewing

- Resolving conflict

- Creating alignment and engagement

- Increasing motivation or leadership

- Getting others out of Critter State

- Giving sensitive performance feedback

- Engaging in sales conversations and marketing messaging

Meta Programs are so sophisticated that most people find it beneficial to review multiple examples and practical exercises to reinforce their understanding. The more you practice these techniques, the more your communication and influence will improve.

Meta Program Objective: Effective Team Communication

Using Meta Programs in messaging can be a powerfully effective way to create emotional agility in both parties. Here's the process we teach clients when crafting powerful communications:

1. Determine the Meta Programs of the people you want to influence. (See the Decoder Questions in the discussion following the heading "The Six Primary Meta Programs" earlier in the chapter.)

2. What do they want most: safety, belonging, or mattering? (See the Safety, Belonging, and Mattering Behavior Decoder in Table 7.1.)

3. What behavior would you like to create in them or change?

4. If the context for your message is leadership, you'll want to consider using an Influencing Phrase (as also given earlier in the chapter):

   - **"I need your help."** Powerfully enrolling. The dominant person becomes small; the subordinate person becomes big.

   - **"What if . . . ?"** Engages the other party and helps make it his or her idea.

   - **"Would it be helpful if . . . ?"** Helps shift someone from Critter State to Smart State and activates problem-solving functions of prefrontal cortex.

   - **"Can you help me understand . . . ?"** Helps you get more clarity without judgment.

5. Craft message.

Here are a few client scenarios where understanding and speaking in the recipients' Meta Programs yielded terrific results.

You'll note that we differentiate between the *Influencer*, the person delivering the message, and the *Influencee*, the person receiving the message, according to both their Meta Programs (MP Profile) and what they most crave (SBM Trigger).

If you already have rapport and basic trust with the Influencee, you'll likely achieve success with one to three Meta Program messages. If there is no rapport—or worse, there is disconnection, anger, or distrust—you'll need five or more messages. The first few will be to simply get you on their map, and then you'll have a chance to enroll them.

Ideally, you'll have three phrases or words that activate their SBM Triggers. For example, if the Influencees crave mattering, to activate their sense of mattering, you may want to say (1) you see them as a thought leader or key player, (2) you need their help, and (3) you want to know what they think.

Scenario 1. Partner at Law Practice Wants Protégé to Lead More Proactively

Tom, a partner at a major Los Angeles–based law firm, wants his protégé Thad to step up. In a coaching session, Tom let me know he needed help with Thad pronto. First, we did a quick Outcome Frame:

1. What would you like? (outcome)

   Instill a greater sense of urgency in Thad; get him to own projects more fully.

2. What will having that do for you? (benefit)

   Less stress, less to follow up on; Thad develops faster; clients get better results and responses.

3. How will you know when you have it? (proof)

   Thad proactively crafts and communicates his plan and timeline, and he owns checking in regarding status—fully taking charge of projects and leading them all the way through.

4. What of value might you risk or lose? What side effects may occur? (what you will have to let go of)

   Will have to let go of some control; will have to resist temptation to dive in and fix things; will have to give Thad more frequent feedback in the beginning.

5. What are your next steps?

   Lay out timeline for change and Thad's specific additional responsibilities; define success; meet with Thad to hand off work and to set up regular check-in and course-correction meetings.

Then we crafted the following message together, taking into account Tom and Thad's MP Profiles and SBM Triggers and using influencing language:

MP Profile and SBM Trigger of Tom (the Influencer): Away, Procedures, General-Specific, Active, *Belonging.*

MP Profile and SBM Trigger of Thad (the Influencee): Away, Procedures, Specific, Reflective, *Mattering*.

Influencing Language Message

"I need your help [Influencing Phrase for becoming subordinate and letting Thad become "bigger" emotionally and feel more powerful]. Thanks to you [Mattering] we solved some key problems [Away] that enabled us to rock last quarter [Mattering]. I've been thinking about [Reflective] how we can improve our process [Procedures] even more.

"What if [Influencing Phrase to propose idea without ego or emotion and to hand off ownership] we were to create a specific process [Specific, Procedures] for crafting client project plans and timelines, communicating status regularly, and driving projects [Specific, Reflective] to completion?

"I think you're the exact guy to own this challenge [Mattering, Away]. What do you think? [Reflective] Could you sketch out a draft plan [Procedures, Specific] for me by _____ [date] at ___ [time]?" [Always have a deadline for a Reflective person!]

Outcome: With this one message, delivered in person and then repeated in summary form in an e-mail, Tom got the result he wanted: Thad stepped up, and Tom got 10 more hours per week to focus on strategic work.

Scenario 2. Help Two Peers Collaborate More Effectively

Lee needed to help her two direct reports Greg and Chan understand how they were clashing, take responsibility for their behaviors, and shift to a more positive state. Greg was the night leader for the factory and had a smaller team than Chan. He would leave work incomplete at the end of his shift and expect Chan's team to finish it. Chan would complain to Lee that Greg was dropping the ball and that his team had to pick up Greg's team's slack. Both were in victim mode with each other, and Chan also slid into rescue mode by doing Greg's work. Chan felt Greg was persecuting him; Greg saw the excessive workload as the persecutor. In a coaching session, we mapped out a plan as well as some Meta Program–based messages.

Step 1 of our plan was for Lee to meet separately with Greg and Chan and help them shift from focusing on the problem and instead focus on the outcome they wanted to create. She had each do an Outcome Frame. She then helped them understand the roles each had been playing (victim, rescuer, and persecutor).[3]

Step 2 was to craft and deliver individual messages to Greg and Chan. She began with Greg:

MP Profile and SBM Trigger of Greg (the Influencee): Toward, Active, Procedures, Specific, *Mattering, Belonging.*

Behavior to Inspire or Change: Collaborate with Chan and his team and see that it's his job to elevate and cultivate others.

Influencing Language Message

"Thanks for your insights [Mattering] on the opportunity we have [Toward] with connecting our night and day teams [Active, Belonging, Specific]. What if [Influencing Phrase to propose idea without ego or emotion and hand off ownership] we were to create a plan [Active, Procedures] for our teams to collaborate [Belonging] more effectively [Mattering]?

"Would it be helpful if [Influencing Phrase to stimulate idea generation, move a person into his or her Smart State] we met for an hour [Active, Belonging, Specific] on _____ [date and time] [Specific] to brainstorm how to set clear expectations and communication between the two teams [Active, Belonging, Mattering, Specific]? I know we can make a positive difference here [Active, Belonging, Mattering]."

Then she met with Chan, the day manager who had a larger team, and she repeated the process. He was the more junior of the two leaders and had really stepped up recently:

MP Profile and SBM Trigger of Chan (the Influencee): Away, Reflective, Options, General, *Safety, Belonging.*

Behavior to Inspire or Change: Collaborate with Greg and his team and solve the problem.

Influencing Language Message

"I need your help [Influencing Phrase for becoming subordinate and letting Chan become "bigger" emotionally and to feel more powerful]. I've been thinking about the issues [Reflective, General, Away, Safety] we're having between the day and night teams and the stress they are causing [Belonging, Safety, Away].

"Can you help me understand [Influencing Phrase to get clarity without judgment or accusation] what choices [Options] we have to bring the teams together [belonging], to bring more stability [Safety] to their relationship [Belonging]? I'd love to hear your ideas [Options, Away, Reflective] on how we can work better together [General, Belonging, Away, Safety]."

Outcome: Thanks to Lee's perseverance and Greg's and Chan's dedication to organization, the above messages worked really well. Greg and Chan actually formed a team and developed new standards for communication, expectation setting, and performance goals, and both teams see themselves now as one. The quality, follow-through, and finger-pointing problems they used to have are now a distant memory.

Meta Programs Objective: Hire the Right Fit for the Role

Meta Programs can also be extremely useful when recruiting and planning your organizational chart. Here are two examples for using this tool to increase emotional agility in these roles.

Consider the following interview questions in your recruiting process. These are self-revealing questions to find out who the person truly is. You will, of course, have your own specific skills-based questions (and if you don't, we have some in the *SmartTribes Playbook* at www.SmartTribes Institute.com/stp).

Scenario 1. Hire Executive Assistant

One of our clients had a dreadful time finding the right executive assistant (EA) for the super-Active, Options, Toward, External CEO. After four failed attempts, we insisted they let us help! In a coaching session with the

CEO and VP of operations, we hashed out the following MP Profile and SBM Trigger that would work best for the role:

Away: This role was about solving or preventing problems and ensuring that the CEO's time was managed optimally.

Procedures: The organization had a number of standard operating procedures (SOPs) that worked well—as long as they were utilized.

Specific: This role was *all* about the details. Tons of details, details that changed, details that we didn't even know we needed. Specificity was essential.

Reflective: It was essential that the EA thought through matters carefully and paid attention to due diligence matters before taking action because there were many potential repercussions from any actions taken by the CEO.

Belonging: This role needed to want to belong with the CEO, to understand what it was like to be the CEO, to empathize and "walk a mile in his or her shoes." This would ensure that the CEO was cared for appropriately and that the EA and CEO were a tight-knit team.

Scenario 2. Hire Salesperson

For sales roles, our clients often find that an SBM Trigger of belonging or mattering, combined with the Meta Programs of Toward, Active, and External, contributes significantly to salespeople's success. Note that the Meta Program combo of Away, Reflective, and Procedures can be indicators that candidates could be terrific at account management or client care—so if they click with your organization's values but don't fit the sales profile, it's worth it to consider them for other client-facing roles.

To Discover the SBM Trigger of Your Candidate

Ask: What is most important to you at work? Please list in order of importance:

- You're in a team that has a plan, and people have your back. (safety)

- You're part of the team, and you have equal value to others. (belonging)

- You're acknowledged and appreciated for your unique contributions, and you are making a difference. (mattering)

To Discover the Meta Program Profile of Your Candidate

Ask: What do you enjoy most at work? What makes work fulfilling? Why?

- Listen for achieving goals and accomplishment [Toward] **or** solving problems and mitigating risk [Away].

Ask: Think of a recent large purchase (such as a car or a home) or a big decision you made recently. Why did you choose the specific item you chose?

- Listen for having lots of options, choices, and possibilities [Options] **or** having a proven process **or** a story that had a number of steps that ended with the choice being made [Procedures].

Ask: Tell me about your weekend.

- Listen for a high-level, net-net executive summary [General] **or** details and specificity [Specific].

Ask: What's your approach when solving problems? How do you decide what to do? How do you do it?

- Listen for take action, charge forward, do it now, and high bias to action [Active] **or** consider, ponder, understand, and analyze and *then* take action [Reflective].

Ask: How do you know you've done a good job?

- Listen for external proof: achieve quota, win the contest, get praise from boss [External] **or** "It's a feeling, I know I've done my best" [Internal].

Please also see the Recruiting Process in this chapter's resources section on www.PowerYourTribe.com.

Meta Program Objective: Close More Sales Faster

Many of our clients seek us out for help crafting Meta Program messages in sales and marketing scenarios. Here are a few examples.

The goal was to send an e-mail that would compel the recipient to agree to a meeting with our client. The CEO sent me the "Before" e-mail draft:

E-mail Draft Before the Meta Program Makeover

Subject: Thank you for attending our conference reception!

Dear X,

Thank you for investing your time to attend our reception during the recent XYZ Conference. It was a pleasure meeting with you. We trust you enjoyed our entertaining guest speaker, Dr. Y, and his informative and unfettered presentation.

If there is anything I can do to assist you, or if you have any questions, please contact me.

Sincerely,

CEO

MP Profile and SBM Trigger of the Participants (the Influencees): Away-Toward, Procedures, Active-Reflective, General, *Mattering*.

The CEO and I edited this message over e-mail back and forth. Notice that when you have a blend of different Meta Programs, you need to use them all, and since the brain deletes information not relevant to it, it actually works:

E-mail Draft After the Meta Program Makeover

Dear [first name],

<u>Thank you for joining us</u> [Mattering] at "An Evening with Dr. Y" at our reception at the XYZ Conference. <u>The energy</u>

in the room was exciting [Active, Toward], Dr. Y delivered a powerful message [Active], and your thought-provoking and insightful questions and comments [Mattering, Reflective, Active] before, during, and after the presentation were much appreciated [Mattering].

Hearing firsthand about the challenges and opportunities [Away, Toward, General] facing your organization helps us develop products and services that help you achieve your goals [Active, Toward, Mattering].

Many attendees expressed interest in learning more [Toward, Away, Active, Reflective, General] about the best practices [Procedures] of successful investment planning [General]. We find having the top five factors in place makes all the difference [Procedures, Mattering]:

[five factors listed here in a numbered list—Procedures]

Our team will be reaching out to you [Active, Mattering] in the next week to send you the photos from the event [Mattering] and to discuss your investment strategy [Away, Toward, Active, Reflective] and share best practices [Procedures] from our most successful clients [Mattering, Toward].

Thanks for being an investment thought leader [Mattering]. We need more like you. [Mattering].

Warmest regards,

CEO

Outcome: Twenty percent of the recipients *reached out to our client* to seek a follow-up conversation before a salesperson could reach out to them! This response rate was a new record for the organization.

You'll find many more examples of using Meta Programs in sales, marketing, CEO, and board scenarios in Chapter 7 of *SmartTribes*.

You'll probably need to use Meta Program–based communications only a few times to get the behavior change going. Then you can use any other tools in this book to move the change forward. Be patient as you learn Meta Programs because we generally teach them in a daylong intensive session and then coach our clients on how to apply them over the course of several sessions. The investment in learning how to speak in Meta Programs in sales, marketing, and leadership scenarios is well worth it, though!

The best part about Meta Programs is that they help us honor and appreciate the experience of another person—and appreciation is the highest form of rapport. Safety, belonging, and mattering, as well as Meta Programs, help us understand what it's like to be other people and to see their map. When we can fully appreciate and be 100 percent present to their experience (to the greatest degree possible without being them!), we profoundly raise the bar on our connection with them. They feel fully seen and understood.

> *Appreciate* doesn't mean approve. Instead, it is from the Latin *ad* (to, toward) + *pretius* (price)—that is, to grasp the nature of or the significance of, or to value highly.

One final thought on communicating using SBM Triggers and Meta Programs: if you're communicating to a group, speak in a blend of the SBM Triggers you think are in the crowd as well as the Meta Programs. Note how we did this in the e-mail text above for the investment client. Since the brain deletes, distorts, and generalizes, the recipients will focus on the message that resonates with them.

The SBM tools and Meta Programs are powerful ways to influence and redirect behavior in the workplace. However, in some extreme cases, there are personality types for which the SBM Index and Meta Programs are insufficient, such as dealing with extreme narcissists who are in positions of leadership and abusing their power. In Part III, Chapter 10, we will cover some breakthrough ways to work with these personalities. In the meantime, we'll discuss bias, borderline behavior, and other blocks to trust in the next chapter—and how to overcome them to build your overall tribal agility.

SUMMARY

1. Communication is about engagement, not manipulation. Words can be used to increase safety, belonging, and mattering in your organization,

and the SBM Behavior Decoder and SBM Communication tools are great ways to help you achieve this.

2. The SBM Index is a swift and effective diagnostic tool for employee engagement. It gives us a clear measurable assessment of what the emotional experience is of the employees within an organization in terms of safety, belonging, and mattering.

3. Meta Programs provide powerful insights into how people communicate, process information, and behave in life and work. Using them, we can understand what roles people would be best suited to and what they crave and need specifically, and we'll know how to communicate with them so they get what they want.

TWITTER TAKEAWAYS

- Often leaders are focusing so intensely on growth that we miss that our team's emotional experience is suffering.

- When we communicate effectively to give people what they crave, the results are remarkable—and swift.

- When we understand people's Meta Programs, we understand their belief systems and how they structure—in part—their identity.

- Meta Programs are the filters through which we see the world—that is, they are the ways our brains process information and determine how we react to it.

- The best part about Meta Programs is that they help us honor and appreciate the experience of other people.

RESOURCES

See this chapter's section on www.PowerYourTribe.com for the following:

- Chapter *Quick Take* video

- STI Recruiting Process: This will save you over 60 hours per candidate!

- SBM Index Recommended Tools and Process

- Convincer Meta Program Information: Key for Sales, Marketing, Business Development Communication, and Content Marketing Strategy

- Meta Program Cliff Notes: Especially Valuable to Sales and Marketing

CHAPTER 8

Build Tribal Agility

Help your team build trust and keep the change going, and increase emotional agility in yourself and others.

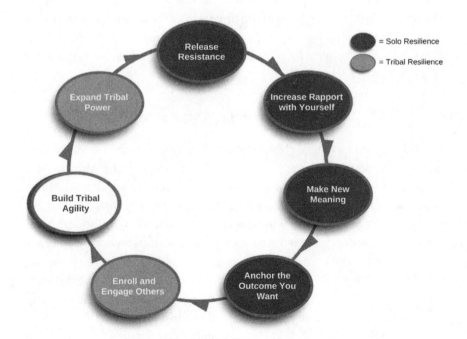

Figure 8.1 The Resilience Cycle: Build Tribal Agility

PROBLEM

This legendary manufacturing organization's product is a commodity, yet the company refuses to be lumped into the dreaded "vendor" bucket. Vendors compete on price, vendors have no leverage, and vendors don't have intellectual property. The team at this family business had built a solid nine figures in annual revenue, with a profit margin that would make any CFO celebrate. Sure, members of the team dive into Critter State sometimes, but they bounce back higher and harder and faster than their competitors do because they are quick to name their emotions due to learned self-awareness and they regulate their emotions as well.

What was the "problem"? There wasn't really one per se. The CEO had reached out to us because he feared complacency—things had been going so well that he wanted to keep his team hungry, eager, and excited to grow. They had made a few high-profile new hires who had felt excluded from the "in" crowd and who had a hard time belonging in this somewhat closed culture. The old-timers figured they had created all the success that the "newbies" were now enjoying. The division into camps had started. To make matters more interesting, one of the top producers in the organization had a borderline personality—he had a tremendous sense of entitlement, even beyond that of the in crowd. This further alienated the new team members and made trust tricky.

PROMISE

Do old-timers get special treatment at your organization? Have you ever had such a great run of success that you thought your team might be getting complacent? The only thing we saw missing was some cultural optimization, which we could address with a little executive coaching.

Since the organization was now headed to the $250 million revenue inflection point, they'd be hiring a lot of new staff. How would they integrate with this culture of cowboys and cowgirls? They had historically hired people "like them." Now, for the organization's health, some diversity would be essential with the help of Bias Navigation tools. Also, it was time to address the challenging personality of the top producer. We'd use the Borderline Behavior Quiz and Decoder, and we'd reinforce trust and tribe with a Cultural GAME Plan.

RESULT

Fast-forward nine months, and many of the key components of the GAME Plan are in place. Fifteen percent of the organization is composed of new hires, so it is essential to keep the GAME Plan in place going forward. Communication is high, and team members and leaders check in with each other often, using SBM tools and the Outcome Frame to make sure relationships are strong, trusting, and on track. They know communication can get them through anything—so they talk through their challenges to keep them from getting blown out of proportion. They know that the differences and diversity among the employees who make up the tribe are essential in order for the organization as a whole to see new points of view, to expose blind spots, and to expand vision. They make lemons into lemonade, and they make the meaning they want constantly.

They talk about leadership all the time. The most promising managers are cultivated in a Leadership Development Program we customized for their culture. If a crisis arises, they form a SWAT team and deal with it swiftly. They know they have one another's back. They are in this together. They exude tribal agility.

Even when the most emotionally agile people come together, they sometimes have conflicts or challenges. Sometimes we bump up against one another or rub each other the wrong way. This is one way we grow. Steve Jobs had a story that illustrated this well:

> When I was a young kid there was a widowed man that lived up the street. He was in his eighties. He was a little scary looking. And I got to know him a little bit. I think he may have paid me to mow his lawn or something.
>
> And one day he said to me, "Come on into my garage, I want to show you something." And he pulled out this dusty old rock tumbler. It was a motor and a coffee can and a little band between them. And he said, "Come on with me." We went out into the back, and we got just some rocks. Some regular old ugly rocks. And we put them in the can with a little bit of liquid and a little bit of grit powder, and we closed the can up and he turned this motor on, and he said, "Come back tomorrow."
>
> And this can was making a racket as the stones went around.

And I came back the next day, and we opened the can. And we took out these amazingly beautiful polished rocks. The same common stones that had gone in, through rubbing against each other like this [clapping his hands], creating a little bit of friction, creating a little bit of noise, had come out these beautiful polished rocks.

That's always been in my mind my metaphor for a team working really hard on something they're passionate about. It's that through the team, through that group of incredibly talented people bumping up against each other, having arguments, having fights sometimes, making some noise, and working together they polish each other and they polish the ideas, and what comes out are these really beautiful stones.[1]

To stick together and build tribal agility through this sometimes uncomfortable process, we'll need some tools to help us. And we'll start with Bias Navigation.

BIAS NAVIGATION: WE'RE ALL A LITTLE BIT BIASED

Before we dive into this key topic, let's do a little lab we learned from Scott Horton.[2]

Make a vertical list of the top 10 people you trust most in your life. Try to list as many as possible from work, and then if or when you run out, list family and friends. Now, next to their name (see the template in Table 8.1), list their gender, race or ethnicity, age, sexual orientation, whether they have a physical disability, and their marital status. Now note the degree of "sameness" across the rows. This is what we call the *like-me bias*.

The Like-Me Bias

The like-me bias is one of the prevalent unconscious biases we see in organizations, and it simply means we feel more safety, belonging, and mattering with people who are like us. That's reasonable; we share the same tribe.

All human beings are biased. It's a natural state of the brain that evolved from the days when we needed to be able to calculate very quickly if

TABLE 8.1 The Trusted 10

First Name or Initials	Gender	Race or Ethnicity	Age	Sexual Orientation	Education	Disability, Yes or No	Marital Status
1							
2							
3							
4							
5							
6							
7							
8							
9							
10							

Source: Adapted from Scott Horton's unconscious bias exercise, https://www.youtube.com /watch?v=i_52T8ufdZM.

someone was like us and thus friendly or unlike us and possibly dangerous. In fact, the brain has far more (three to four times as much!) real estate devoted to identifying threats than to identifying opportunities and rewards. There are over 150 different types of biases—and all have their roots in the structure of the brain.

Biases are part of what keeps us sane and able to process the enormous amount of information we are bombarded with at any point in time. If we were not able to form unconscious biases and delete, distort, and generalize accordingly, we would probably go crazy pretty darned fast.

Since we are all naturally biased, there's no need to feel ashamed of it. However, there's a very profound business case for ensuring that we mitigate or entirely remove our biases in certain situations. That's where Bias Navigation can help.

For example, think about *how* people moved into your inner circle, your "trusted 10." What made you trust them? Shared experiences? Similarity? What else?

Stepping back a bit, think about the organizational effect of the like-me bias over time. Are we more likely to hire people like us? Being "same as" increases our sense of belonging, but what happens when *everyone* is like us? How do we get profoundly different perspectives? How do we innovate? Will we be able to "bump up against one another" to grow? Or will we get along too well to challenge our growth and status quo? How does bias affect emotional agility?

The Importance of Inclusion

Many people think that diversity is simply about having a diverse team, one that has representatives from different genders, races, and ethnicities. Although that is a start, according to Vernā Myers, "Diversity is being invited to the party. Inclusion is being asked to dance."[3]

Let's take a look at this issue from the perspective of your "not-like-you" team members. Human infants have a very long period of being dependent on the adults of their "tribe." We instinctually mirror the behaviors of others from birth in order to belong and therefore survive, and if we are socially ostracized from the group, we feel physical pain.

When our belonging is threatened, when we are ostracized or excluded, we enter Critter State—our brain literally cannot function the way it does when it feels safe and is in Smart State. Specifically, we release an enzyme that attacks the hippocampus, which is responsible for regulating synapses,[4] and as a result our brain does the following:

- Reduces the field of view and focuses only on a narrow span of what it must do to survive. Myelin sheathing (see Chapter 9) increases on existing neural pathways, and we are less likely to try new solutions.

- Shrinks its working memory so that it is not distracted by other ideas, bits of information, or stray thoughts. This means we can't problem solve optimally. Think of students panicked by a pop quiz: the information is there, but they cannot access it.

- Is less creative. With less gray matter and modified synapses, we experience fewer ideas, thoughts, and information available to "bump into each other," so our capacity to create is reduced.

- Increases cell density in the amygdala, the area of the brain responsible for fear processing and threat perception, making us more likely to be reactive rather than self-controlled.

- Is less likely to connect with others. Fight, flight, freeze, or faint is not a "sharing" type of activity. When the synapses have been modified in this way, we appear grumpy and unsociable.

What's the return on investment (ROI) of diversity and inclusion?

- Increased safety, belonging, and mattering
- Increased collective intelligence
- Greater innovation from diverse points of view
- Easier and more diverse recruiting
- A culture of meritocracy that creates empowerment

Neuroscientists have repeatedly proven that teams with diversity and inclusion *vastly outperform* homogeneous teams. Period.

As leaders, we must promote everyone's Smart State by not just hiring diverse team members but *including* them. If your not-like-you team members don't feel included, they'll end up in Critter State, and no one gets the benefits of diversity. But here's the catch:

Humans rarely communicate as clearly as they think they do!

We addressed this topic in Chapter 7, when we discussed the experience of "same as" and Meta Programs. It's actually quite a miracle that we understand anything about each other. How many times a week, a day, or even an hour have you thought you were understood but later discovered a complete disconnect?

Everyone has his or her unique way of communicating. To truly promote diversity and inclusion, it is absolutely critical to train your team in effective communication skills. Awareness alone doesn't work, but structures that prevent biases and build effective communication patterns and habits do. That's what will allow people to get to know one another as individuals, not as ethnic, racial, or gender groups. That's what will bust the like-me bias.

Here are some specific Like-Me Bias Navigation tools.

Tool: Three-Minute Journal

Think of a person who is different from you and on the outside of a group you are in. For one week, journal for three minutes every day about how that person is like you. At the end of the week, reflect for a few moments on how your perspective might have changed.

Tool: Add Diversity, Equity, and Inclusion Structures

Assess your organization's current structures: How do you choose who gets what assignment? Who gets promoted? Who is invited to meetings? Consider developing someone who is not like you by giving that person explicit opportunities:

- **Example 1:** Some orchestras now hold auditions behind screens, after they noticed that many people selected were similar to one another in ways that were irrelevant to their musical talents and proficiencies.

- **Example 2:** When making project assignments, pay attention to who gets picked based on what criteria and then level the playing field. Also, consider providing mentoring programs people may apply for.

Cognitive Biases

In addition to the like-me bias, there is a handful of other prevalent unconscious biases we categorize as cognitive biases. *Cognitive bias* refers to the systematic pattern of deviation from norms or rationales in making judgments. These biases cause conclusions, inferences, and assumptions about people and situations to be drawn in a less than logical fashion. We all create our own "subjective social reality" from our perception of the input we receive—both from outside of us and from inside of us. The trouble is that biases, whether cognitive or like me, damage safety, belonging, and mattering, and they create the experience of unfairness. Unfairness then leads to Critter State, and emotional agility is dramatically reduced.

Neil Jacobstein, an expert in artificial intelligence, notes that we use artificial intelligence (AI) and algorithms to address many cognitive biases, such as the following:

- **Anchoring bias:** Inclination to focus on a specific piece of information or attribute when making decisions. This information or attribute becomes one's "anchor."

- **Availability bias:** Inclination to overemphasize the probability of certain events. Whatever is overemphasized has greater "availability" in one's memory, whether it is positive or negative.

- **Bandwagon effect:** Inclination to "jump on the bandwagon" and respond with herd mentality. One does or believes something because many people do.

- **Hindsight bias:** Inclination to see past events as having been predictable at the time those events occurred. This has an "I knew it all along" effect.

- **Normalcy bias:** Inclination to resist reacting to or planning for a disaster. One of the contributors to denial, this bias results in one "normalizing" something that is *not* normal.

- **Optimism bias:** Inclination toward expecting favorable and pleasing outcomes. This bias causes people to be overly optimistic without data to back up that expectation.

- **Planning fallacy bias:** Inclination to underestimate costs and timelines and overestimate benefits. Consequently, planning is incomplete or inaccurate.

- **Sunk-cost or loss-aversion bias:** Inclination to see more value in giving something up than in acquiring it. Thus, one might quit too soon or miss opportunities.[5]

Which of those biases do you recognize in yourself?

Tool: Cognitive Bias Navigation

To optimize emotional agility, innovation, and business growth, first notice where your biases often are, then recognize which ones are relevant in a given scenario, and then use practical strategies to navigate those biases. Check out this challenge an executive coaching client recently had, and then we'll summarize the steps for navigating cognitive bias.

Our client needed to hire a VP of marketing to take the organization to the next level. He had four candidates who had made it to the interview stage, and one had even made an on-site visit to meet with four different key stakeholders in the organization. I asked the VP why he favored this one candidate by such a long shot. As I listened, I heard the following biases:

- **Planning fallacy bias:** The client underestimated how long the process would take and what a great hire would cost (that is, he was thinking the process would take a few weeks versus a few months).

- **Anchoring bias:** This client focused on one piece of information (the candidate's current job accomplishments) rather than the big picture (his résumé had two decades of one- to two-year roles—a red flag that our client's bias missed).

- **Availability bias:** Because the candidate was successful in his current situation (a huge organization with tons of resources available), the client assumed he'd be successful in a much smaller organization (with about one-sixth of the resources the candidate was accustomed to).

- **Optimism bias:** Yep, some of this too. The client thought he'd have a solid candidate identified, screened, and hired within six weeks.

I expressed these concerns, and I explained how cognitive biases can be busted:

1. **Take your time.** You will make better decisions when you aren't hungry, tired, or stressed. Taking time before making a decision allows you to think about the future and the impact of your decision.

2. **Get an outside view.** Ask trusted advisors or peers for their opinion.

3. **Consider other options.** What else could you do?

Then the VP asked me to interview the candidate. I deeply questioned the candidate in each of the bias areas our client had. The result? This candidate was not the right fit for the organization. Not by a long shot. The good news was that our client avoided a costly hiring mistake, and the better news was that he still had three candidates who could fit the bill.

The story ended with him hiring a candidate who was not like the VP (thereby effectively busting this bias too!). She is doing a great job, and all are thrilled with the good hire.

• • •

Once we create a base of trust with Bias Navigation, we can then build on that trust by addressing any borderline behavior.

BORDERLINE BEHAVIOR NAVIGATION: HOW TO SURVIVE BULLIES AND NARCISSISTS AT WORK

We're hearing a lot about psychological safety, narcissism, and subconscious bias in the workplace lately. But what's beneath many of these challenges is the borderline personality disorder (BPD)—a topic many tread lightly around. We do so because unlike anxiety, depression, bipolar, or other diagnoses, borderline isn't easily treatable or curable. I do not profess to be an expert here, so please note that diagnosis should be left to the appropriate medical professionals.

Very few people are diagnosed with this very difficult condition as "true" borderlines. The truth is that we all exhibit some borderline behavior, especially when we are under great stress. So bear this in mind as you read on.

Here's what BPD is and how it's part of your work and life. Then we'll talk about how to deal with BPD and borderline behavior in the workplace.

What Is Borderline Personality Disorder?

The *Diagnostic and Statistical Manual of Mental Disorders* (DSM) has a long list of criteria for BPD. Here are the ones you'll most likely see in the workplace:

1. Frantic efforts to avoid real or imagined abandonment

2. A pattern of unstable and intense relationships

3. Unstable self-image or sense of self

4. Intense moodiness or rapid mood changes

5. Inappropriate, intense anger

6. Stress-induced paranoid thoughts or dissociative symptoms (loses touch with reality)

We all know someone who fits those criteria. According to Christine Ann Lawson's work, people suffering from BPD have suffered one or more of the following traumas in their past:

- Inadequate emotional support following parental abandonment (through death or divorce)

- Parental abuse, emotional neglect, or chronic denigration

- Being labeled as the "no good" child by a borderline mother[6]

When children suffer one of the above, their ability to attach in a healthy way is damaged. Then we'll see anxiety, avoidance, ambivalence or resistance, or disorganization in their experience of attaching to others. According to Christine Lawson, there are four types of borderline personalities:

1. **Waif:** This person is helpless, sad, and lonely and feels like a victim. Waifs try to get others to give them sympathy and caregiving. They can be socially engaging, then turn on you, seek help and then reject it, and give away, lose, or destroy good things. Their mantra is "Life is way too hard." When you have Waifs in the office, they'll be emotionally exhausting and frustrating to be around.

2. **Hermit:** This person lives in fear of threat and persecution from a dangerous world. Hermits try to get others to share their anxiety and need for protection. They are perfectionists and worriers, and if you misstep, they'll shut you out. Their mantra is "Life is too dangerous." When you have Hermits in the workplace, you'll want to follow in their path in order to clear up the fear they are spreading before your team's performance is affected.

3. **Queen or King:** This person feels empty, deprived, and angry and has an insatiable longing that cannot be fulfilled. Kings and Queens are demanding, flamboyant, and intimidating, and they feel entitled to invade the boundaries of others. They can appear all-powerful,

and they do not like it when others question them. They want others to comply. Period. Their mantra is "Life is all about me and should be even more about me. I am important, and you are not." Having Queens or Kings in the office is tough—they'll make others feel inferior and dismissed.

4. **Witch or Warlock:** This person feels self-hatred and the conviction that he or she is evil. Witches and Warlocks need power and control over others in order to prop up their basic self-esteem. The more fear and submission they can get from others, the more self-importance they derive. They are domineering; you'll see them rage and violate the boundaries of others. Hostility masks their fear. Their mantra is "Life is war." Witches and Warlocks are often the trickiest personalities to deal with because they're just plain dark and emotionally volatile.[7]

I'll bet you've seen some of these qualities in many people you know—including yourself. That's because we're all a little borderline.

We're All a Little Bit Borderline

In borderline behavior, there are always two roles: the *borderline primary* (they're "pitching") and the *borderline secondary* (they're "catching"). In families, parents usually are primary and kids are secondary. At work, the roles aren't always as clear.

Who exhibits borderline behavior in your life? Do you slide into the secondary role and get swept up in their drama? When are you the primary?

The tricky part about primary borderline behavior is the stance of perpetual innocence, as well as the need to win no matter what—even at the risk of damaging relationships. That's the system you're working in when you play on this field. Borderlines will also try to "recruit" you to play with them, to try to push your buttons and make you angry, to get you to sympathize and take sides, even to try to get you to fire them in extreme cases.

Bullies who are truly borderline are often the most severe cases you can deal with. So it is wise to be cautious here. We cannot simply provide more safety, belonging, and mattering to help shift them from tension to empowerment. For true borderlines, it is *unavailable.*

Tool: Borderline Behavior Quiz

Table 8.2 is a quiz we use to guesstimate the type of borderline personalities our clients are dealing with. For each significant relationship in your workplace (for example, your boss or a colleague), put a check mark by any of the statements that seem to characterize the person's behavior. And in addition, if *you* say or think any of these things, put an X mark by it. Then you can reflect on where *you* learned this behavior.

TABLE 8.2 Borderline Behavior Quiz

You deserve the best, but I deserve better.	
You'll never escape my control.	
Nobody cares about me.	
I am a special exception.	
You are so lucky.	
It's never good enough.	
You're going to get hurt!	
The rules don't apply to me.	
You've done it now!	
It's never enough.	
You'll be sorry.	
They're out to get us!	
You deserve to suffer.	
What's the matter with you?	
Something terrible just happened! (when she lost her reading glasses)	
What's mine is mine, and what's yours is mine.	
Don't need me because I can't help you.	
I feel used.	
I deserve more.	

My life is so much worse than yours.	
Keep your doors locked!	
You won't get away with this.	
I could kill you.	
Act like everything is fine.	
Let me do that for you.	

Source: Derived from Christine Lawson's work with additions by NLP Marin and SmartTribes Institute.

Tool: Borderline Behavior Decoder

Table 8.3 is the Borderline Behavior Decoder for the quiz in Table 8.2. This decoder isn't intended to label or ostracize. It's about understanding. Approach these scenarios with compassion, kindness, and, yes, caution.

TABLE 8.3 Borderline Behavior Decoder

Note: WF = Waif, H = Hermit, Q = Queen, and W = Witch.

Q	You deserve the best, but I deserve better.	
W	You'll never escape my control.	
WF	Nobody cares about me.	
Q	I am a special exception.	
WF	You are so lucky.	
Q	It's never good enough.	
H	You're going to get hurt!	
Q	The rules don't apply to me.	
H	You've done it now!	
Q	It's never enough.	
W	You'll be sorry.	
H	They're out to get us!	

W	You deserve to suffer.	
H	What's the matter with you?	
H	Something terrible just happened! (when she lost her reading glasses)	
Q	What's mine is mine, and what's yours is mine.	
WF	Don't need me because I can't help you.	
WF	I feel used.	
Q	I deserve more.	
WF	My life is so much worse than yours.	
W	I could kill you.	
H	Keep your doors locked!	
W	You won't get away with this.	
H	Act like everything is fine.	
WF	Let me do that for you.	

Source: Derived from Christine Lawson's work with additions by NLP Marin and SmartTribes Institute.

Tool: Borderline Behavior Navigation

If you are dealing with true borderlines (people who live permanently in the primary position), here's the bad news: they will always perceive themselves as innocent. They simply *cannot* be wrong or guilty, as they cling to innocence for dear life.

Here's the good news: as the secondary, you have a lot more flexibility in your behavior, meaning you get to choose what you're willing to be guilty of. Yes, you'll likely have an adaptation pattern of behavior in which you sometimes exhibit behaviors similar to those of the primary, but you won't be "all in."

1. Say OWOW
First, the borderlines will likely push many of your buttons at the same time, as that's one of their special gifts. I learned a tool from my mentor

Carl Buchheit that's very helpful when dealing with borderline behavior. The acronym is OWOW because when dealing with the at-times-shocking cruelty of borderlines, you're likely saying, "Oh! Wow!"

O = Oh, my God! (Yes, it's shocking.)

W = What the f*&%! (Yes, it's hurtful.)

O = OK. (Here you are consenting to the fact that this is actually happening.)

W = What would you like? (Complete an Outcome Frame to restore choice to your behavior.) [8]

Now that we have a basic coping strategy in OWOW, let's look at the second strategy: choosing your realm of guilt.

2. Choose Your Realm of Guilt

Let's acknowledge that (until we learn to manage it) the ego is always seeking control or approval. Both of these cause us pain because there is very little one can actually control in life, and seeking approval puts your self-worth in the hands of another. Lose-lose. So let go of having either with a borderline. All you can do is choose your realm of guilt.

To survive and ultimately thrive with a borderline primary (if you can't quit or get transferred to another department), you'll likely be guilty of many things. The key is to retain your sense of self-respect and integrity. Here are some examples of what you'll be "guilty" of in the presence of primary borderlines:

- Standing up for yourself.

- Having healthy boundaries.

- Not responding fast enough: pausing and saying you need time to think. If you continually do not give the primary borderlines immediate gratification, they will find someone else who will!

- Giving in. You may need to do this—be kind to yourself—because it's an unwinnable situation.

- Disengaging. If they are raging, this is your only option—let them wear themselves out.

- Find a way for them to get rid of you while maintaining your integrity (and hopefully getting a nice severance package).

A helpful way to choose your realm or realms of guilt is to select the one or ones that feel OK to you. You may want to start with one and then add another as you learn to navigate interactions with the borderlines. Then it'll get easier, especially the more curious you become.

3. Be Curious

This is like the Anthropologist stance that I described in *SmartTribes*.[9] You are fascinated by the behavior of the borderlines and you want to understand what it's like to be them. Then you can ask one of two questions (or both), taught to me by Matt Kahn (TrueDivineNature.com):

- How may I serve you?

- How may I give you a better experience of me?

In either case, the borderline probably will tell you all the ways you need to change for his or her life to work. This is when you can kindly say something like "Thank you for your feedback" and leave. The list they gave you is what they want to change in *themselves*. You've just experienced a projection. Send them love and step away. They'll get help if or when they want to, but often they don't want to because for primary borderlines, everyone "is messed up" but them.

It's key to remember with compassion that all borderline behavior is an unworkable attempt to manage loss and damage related to low or no love, safety, belonging, or mattering. That's why true borderlines are not capable of deep long-term relationships and cannot be present during intense emotion.

●　●　●

To sum up: Remember that the behaviors of borderline primaries are designed to push people's buttons (anger, helplessness, persuasive charm) in an attempt to avoid real or imagined abandonment. They will draw you in because to them, their life depends on it. Although their attacks will *feel* personal, it's best not to take it that way or you'll find yourself in Critter State before you know it. In Chapter 4, we covered how important it is to distinguish *behavior* from the intention of the behavior so that we can have more choices about how we respond to primary borderlines.

If you ever find your buttons pushed, just take a breath and use OWOW or the Maneuvers of Consciousness process we discussed in Chapter 3 so that you can quickly shift from Critter to Smart State.

Once you use the tools and strategies to become present to any borderline challenges, you're ready for the final piece in your tribal agility strategy: a Cultural GAME Plan to solidify trust and scale your staff.

THE CULTURAL GAME PLAN: CREATE A PASSIONATELY ENGAGED CULTURE

The issue of trust can make or break an organization. A *Harvard Business Review* article states, "People crave transparency, openness, and honesty from their leaders. Unfortunately, business leaders continue to face issues of trust. According to a survey by the American Psychological Association, a quarter of workers say they don't trust their employer, and only about half believe their employer is open and up front with them."[10]

Handling individual bias and borderline issues goes a long way toward building trust. Now it's time to build a *culture* of trust with a strong tribal identity.

The best way to boost revenue, profits, fulfillment, fun, and performance in general is to create an emotionally engaged and emotionally agile cultural identity. If you don't have specific structures to create it, you might be unintentionally disengaging your tribe without even realizing it.

But first: How exactly does engagement work? What happens in the brain when we are engaged?

Engagement comes from feeling good, from passion for the organization, from meaningful work, and from attaching part of one's identity to one's job. And this experience is physiologically created by two neurotransmitters and one hormone:

- **Oxytocin:** A hormone that contributes to the feeling of bonding and connectedness to others

- **Dopamine:** A neurotransmitter with many roles, including signaling cells when the anticipation of reward is present and driving reward-motivated behavior

- **Serotonin:** A neurotransmitter that contributes to good feelings and general well-being

As leaders when we intentionally help the brains of our employees to generate dopamine, serotonin, and oxytocin, we create good feelings for the organization. We create these good feelings via a number of programs in your Cultural GAME Plan which we'll cover in a moment.

First, having a strong mission, vision, and values sets the tone for your tribal purpose and code of conduct (oxytocin). Next, acknowledging employees for being models of your values creates social validation (dopamine and serotonin).

Let's return to the fact that the brain needs structures to connect the heart to the workplace, to bring emotion in, so our teams know we care about them. It's time to dive into your Cultural GAME Plan.

GAME stands for the following:

Growth: How are you helping your team aspire to greater knowledge and capabilities?

Appreciation: How are helping your team feel appreciated and valued?

Measurement: How are you ensuring that your team performs and understands your expectations?

Engagement: How are you helping keep everyone's heart and mind focused on how much they love your organization?

A Cultural GAME Plan provides clear "rules" about how to stay in the tribe (be safe and belong) and gain status (matter) in each of these four key areas. It not only establishes trust at the cultural level, it also provides the most fulfilling work experience, which will yield the happiest and most committed, productive, loyal, long-term, constantly evolving emotionally agile team members. You deserve this. So do they.

Tool: Cultural GAME Plan

Here's the recipe for your Cultural GAME Plan:

1. **Work through an SBM Index to find what your tribe needs (see Chapter 7).**

2. **Create your GAME Plan based on your SBM Index findings.** Your Cultural GAME Plan needs to encompass safety, belonging, and mattering throughout the entire *employee experience* (EX), which means you'll want to include recruiting and onboarding, performance motivation, and ongoing talent optimization. This is how so many of our clients earn Best Places to Work awards—which make a *huge* difference in recruiting, retention, performance, and employee happiness overall.

   What you include in your plan will be customized to your needs, but here are some examples of how to increase SBM through specific structures, tools, and rituals for growth, appreciation, measurement, and engagement. Note how each part of the plan maps to SBM Index results (S for safety, B for belonging, and M for mattering):

   - **Growth:** How are you helping your team aspire to greater knowledge and capabilities?
     - Individual Development Plans (S, B, M)
     - Leadership Lunches (B)
     - Annual (Organization-wide) Learning and Development Plans (S, B, M)
     - Feedback Frames (S, B, M)
     - Turnaround Processes (S, B, M)

   - **Appreciation:** How are helping your team feel appreciated and valued?
     - High Fives (M, B)
     - Rock Star of the Month [M, B]
     - Weekly Wins (S, B, M)
     - Friday Toasts (M, B)
     - Merit Money and/or peer-based bonus programs[11] (B, M)

   - **Measurement:** How are you ensuring that your team performs and understands your expectations?
     - Accountability Structures (S, B, M)
     - Weekly Status (S, M)

- ○ Dashboards (S, B, M)

- ○ Performance Self-Evaluations (S, B, M)

- ○ Engagement Surveys (such as the SBM Index) (S, B, M)

- **Engagement:** How are you helping keep everyone's heart and mind focused on how much they love your organization?

  - ○ Engaging mission, vision, and values statements (S, B, M)

  - ○ Impact Descriptions (S, B, M)

  - ○ Coffee with the CEO program (B, M)

  - ○ Organization-wide contests (M, B)

  - ○ Diversity, Equity, and Inclusion Structures (S, B)

  - ○ Optimal recruiting processes (to ensure value alignment) (B)

  - ○ Optimal onboarding processes (S, B, M)

  - ○ Visual, auditory, and kinesthetic goals (goals you show that people are progressing toward V, talk about A, and anchor in an activity K) (S, B, M)

3. **Implement your GAME Plan on a monthly basis. After the initial programs have been in place for six to nine months, complete a new SBM Index to assess results.** A GAME Plan will span many months or even years as an organization rolls out relevant programs.

   For example, you'll recall the SBM Index results shared in Chapter 7 (Table 7.2). Table 8.4 gives the first month's programs from the client's GAME Plan based on those SBM Index results.

TABLE 8.4 The First Month's SBM Index Programs from the Client's GAME Plan Based on the SBM Index Results in Table 7.2

What	Why (Details)	Benefits	Owner	Budget
Create Culture Team	Cross-functional group of 5 people to be sounding board and support and to roll out culture programs.	Have internal champions, and avoid having programs look like they are "HR sanctioned."	Susanna	NA

What	Why (Details)	Benefits	Owner	Budget
Draft engaging mission, vision, and values	Understand why we're here, where we are going together, and what our tribal behavior code is.	Increased retention, engagement, intrinsic motivation, and safety, belonging, and mattering (SBM).	Tyrone	NA
Create High Five Program, Version 1	Anyone can appreciate or acknowledge someone across the organization for modeling our values. Start with flip charts in the kitchen, then we can get techy later.	More belonging and mattering, values embraced more quickly. Generates good feelings about each other and organization overall.	Susanna	Need SharePoint for Version 2
Weekly Wins	Celebrate the little good things that happen weekly. Provide format for leaders to use with their teams. Submissions due to leaders by 5 p.m. Thursday. Leaders' and talent's rollouts and e-mails sent out each Friday by 2 p.m.	Increased safety, belonging, and mattering.	Susanna	NA, but may use Slack in the future
Accountability Structures, Decision Spaces, and Weekly Status reports	Gain clarity on priorities and performance expectations. Gain visibility on dependencies and contingencies across departments. Start with Google Sheets.	Better decision-making. Everyone knows what they own and when it's due.	Jean-Claude	NA, but may research software later

Note (from Chapter 7) that what the organization craved most overall was belonging, so we put cultural rituals in place first to create connection and tribe. In the following months we would address safety and mattering as the experience of belonging was strengthened. In addition to the initial programs, we coached the investments leader to bring more safety to his team.

4. **As you continue to implement your plan, you'll enjoy increasing amounts of the benefits our clients love:**

    - Increased employee retention by more than 90 percent

    - Increased profit per employee by over 22 percent

    - Increased performance by 35 to 50 percent

    - Increased emotional engagement, agility, and morale by 67 to 100 percent

    - Decreased time to recruit for open positions by more than 50 percent

For our proven templates on all aspects of a GAME Plan (and all the other key best practices and tools for creating a SmartTribe), see the *Smart-Tribes Playbook* at www.SmartTribesInstitute.com/STP.

Once you have your cultural framework, you can further deepen your *emotional* framework beneath your GAME Plan. When you're ready to do so, check out the Tribal Identity resource for this chapter on PowerYour Tribe.com.

When we have strategies in place to address bias, foster inclusion, and navigate borderline personality disorder issues, and when those strategies are supported by a rich Cultural GAME Plan and growing tribal identity, we get team members who say, "I love my job, I trust my leader, and I'm ready to rock today!" This is true emotional agility and engagement.

SUMMARY

1. Working together is like polishing rocks. Team members won't always agree or get along, but in high-performing teams, they bounce back to the Smart State higher, harder, and faster than their competitors do.

2. All human beings are biased. It's a natural state of the brain that evolved from the days when we needed to be able to calculate very quickly if someone was like us and thus friendly or unlike us and possibly dangerous.

3. A diverse group consistently performs better, making it clearly worth our while to figure out the bias conundrum.

4. We all exhibit some borderline behavior, especially when we are under great stress. Dealing with true borderlines requires navigation and survival strategies.

5. The Cultural GAME Plan helps us provide a fulfilling work experience, which will yield the happiest and most committed, productive, loyal, long-term, constantly evolving, and emotionally agile team members.

6. Unpacking the SBM Index results help us create an appropriate GAME Plan. The GAME Plan helps us forge the "rules" for how to belong to the tribe and thus be safe and the "rules" for how to matter and thus gain status in our tribe.

TWITTER TAKEAWAYS

- To truly promote diversity and inclusion, it is absolutely critical to train your team in effective communication skills.

- Neuroscientists have repeatedly proven that teams with diversity and inclusion vastly outperform homogeneous teams. Period.

- All borderline behavior is an unworkable attempt to manage loss and damage related to the lack of love, safety, belonging, or mattering.

- The best way to boost revenue, profits, fulfillment, fun, and performance in general is to create an emotionally engaged culture.

- Are you unintentionally disengaging your tribe? The brain needs structures to connect the heart to the workplace.

RESOURCES

See this chapter's section on www.PowerYourTribe.com for the following:

- Chapter *Quick Take* video
- Diversity, Equity, and Inclusion Optimization: Helpful Practices and Processes
- Tribal Identity Process: How to Forge a Company Personality
- STI Recruiting Process: This will save you over 60 hours per candidate.
- Values Examples

CHAPTER 9

Expand Tribal Power

Help your tribe navigate any obstacle, thrive on feedback, and redefine their personal best.

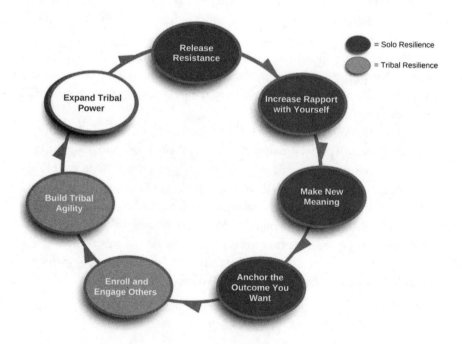

Figure 9.1 The Resilience Cycle: Expand Tribal Power

PROBLEM

Sue, the CMO at a Midwest insurance company, receives a litany of excuses from her VP of marketing when deadlines are missed. And he continues to miss them.

Dan, VP of sales at a Silicon Valley software company, runs himself ragged tracking the performance of his salespeople and cajoling them into using the customer relationship management (CRM) system. He often donates time from his own assistant to do the salespeople's CRM data entry.

Karen, VP of talent at an East Coast professional services firm, has frequent challenges with one of the firm's top consultants. He changes agreements constantly, says he doesn't remember promises made, and even bullies her and her team.

PROMISE

Do any of the above examples resonate with you? Have you experienced similar challenges yourself or witnessed them with others? What do all these leaders have in common?

They're being "inappropriately small" and letting their direct reports become "inappropriately big" by default. They're not owning their role and the power and authority it brings. They're not standing in what we at STI refer to as their *Energetic Weight*.

Energetic Weight is like the foundational components of a building. If one pillar is out of place, the structure gets wobbly. If one pillar is too big or too small, the ceiling tilts and loses balance. If you don't stand in your Energetic Weight, someone else will, or if you're the leader, anarchy will result.

Expanding your tribe's power begins with expanding your own via Energetic Weight. After that, you need to use *Myelination Practice*, the *Feedback Frame*, and possibly other tools such as the Four *Conversations* to get people back to their proper weight. If things still don't improve—which is unlikely—use the *Seven-Step Feedback Frame*.

RESULT

Once I coached the CMO and the VPs to get them back in their Energetic Weight, the results were fantastic.

Sue no longer receives a litany of excuses from her VP of marketing when deadlines are missed. Because he doesn't miss them. He understands now that this isn't OK.

Dan no longer runs himself ragged tracking the performance of his salespeople and cajoling them into using the CRM system. They now understand that if they don't enter the CRM data in a timely manner, they can find a job elsewhere. And his assistant now has time to implement cool sales contests to increase revenue.

Karen let the prima donna consultant go. Her team is much happier now.

You've come a long way! Now that you've reintegrated some wayward parts of yourself, gotten clear on the energetic expense of unhelpful emotions, and have some ability to self-regulate, let's look at how you are showing up for others (and yourself).

ENERGETIC WEIGHT:
THE ART OF SHOWING UP

Everything is energy. Everything. Einstein proved this truth ages ago. Now let's apply it to the world of resilience and leadership. How we "show up" energetically is essential to building healthy teams and companies.

The concept of Energetic Weight is based on psychotherapist Bert Hellinger's revolutionary work on Family Constellations and Systemic Constellations.[1] Today his work is used in numerous transformative applications in relationships, business, politics, and countless disciplines.

In Hellinger's work, he describes *proper weight* as someone occupying his or her appropriate position and role in a system. And each one is unique. For example, in a family system, the child is smaller than the parent; the child takes and the parent gives. Imagine how strange it would be for the child to be the caretaker. It would lead to great dysfunction.

Similarly, in an organization, a new employee has less responsibility and weight than the founding CEO. The employee must not start taking on the role of the CEO, as that wouldn't serve anybody. The CEO, in turn, must not shy away from responsibility and try to have the weight of a new employee.

Energetic Weight is the energy, the power, the authority that comes with a given role. But does the individual with the role choose to use it? Standing in your Energetic Weight is about standing up for what you believe is right, doing the right thing, treating others with respect, and drawing the line when others are not honoring who you are and what your role represents.

You know that people are in their *proper Energetic Weight* when you feel confident about their competence. You experience them as having clarity on what they need to do. And you trust them to get on with it, without feeling compelled to micromanage them.

You know people are in their *improper Energetic Weight* when you feel you need to baby-sit them or you feel repulsed by the way they are trying to do everything else *but* work toward meeting their assigned responsibilities. They often pretend to be expert at things they have no expertise *in*.

Too many leaders, in an attempt to "be nice," to fit in, to be popular, miss the opportunity to stand in their Energetic Weight. Then they wonder why they are mired in low-value activities, why their team doesn't perform, why it's hard to get things done through other people.

Think of Energetic Weight as a mantle you wear or even a crown. When you accept the responsibility of a given role, you "take on," or wear, an energetic mantle of sorts. You agree to hold yourself to a higher standard than your prior role, perhaps, because this new role may convey more authority, carry more responsibility (such as financial accountability or the performance of a larger team). It requires you to ensure that your team honors your weight.

A while back, we had a temporary administrative assistant make a series of travel plan mistakes. They were big—even though my calendar said 9 a.m., the car service to take me to the airport had been told 9 p.m. The temp then got really flustered, so her leader had to dive in to fix things at a level she shouldn't have had to work at. This reduced the leader's Energetic Weight. Next, since the leader's weight had been reduced to clean up this mess, she was now doing more low-value activities than she should've had to do, and this affected her leader. Which was me. So now my Energetic Weight was reduced because I wasn't getting the support I needed.

Make sure your direct reports and their direct reports understand Energetic Weight! My assistant now screens administrative help more diligently for detail orientation, so we reframed this experience to be a learning one.

Tool: Energetic Weight

How is your Energetic Weight? Would you like to increase it?

Here's a quick quiz to provide some insight. Answer yes or no to each of the following questions:

1. I spend 70 percent or more of my time on high-value activities.

2. I hold others accountable to their commitments even if they go into victim or persecutor behavior and try to make me "the bad guy."

3. My team knows what is expected of them, and they come forth when they drop the ball—rarely do I have to mention it.

4. My peers know what to expect in our interactions, what's OK and what's not, and where the line is that they shouldn't cross.

5. My supervisor (or boss or leader) wouldn't dream of delegating work to me that could be given to someone more junior.

6. My team wouldn't dream of bouncing delegated work back to me, their leader.

7. I am known as fair, direct, and collaborative and as a straight shooter. This is why people trust me—I don't play games, I give others credit when due, and I continuously elevate and cultivate others.

8. I see my role as a privilege, not an entitlement. I am here to serve my company's mission, fulfill its vision, honor its values, and make a positive contribution to its clients, partners, and team.

9. I complete the work I am able to complete that is appropriate for my role and the amount of time I dedicate to work. I don't self-sacrifice and work excessive hours—that would reduce my work quality, and it would also mean either I am not delegating enough or I am taking on more work than is healthy or appropriate.

10. I am OK with conflict and stress. If I disagree with something, I say so, in a respectful way, with the reasons why. If others try to shoot down my ideas, I get curious and find out what I may have missed. When under stress, I stay calm and move through it. We're all works in progress, and that's OK. We'll get through it together.

Here's an interpretation of the scores:

0 to 3 yes answers: It's time to get a coach to work on building your Energetic Weight. Start to uncover the stories you're telling yourself about being seen, having power, and claiming your rightful place. It may be time to rewrite them.

4 to 6 yes answers: You're on your way. Hone your skills, expand your heart, ground your energy into the earth, and be the glorious human being you are. Now comes the best part: you get to help others understand this too.

7+ yes answers: Optimization is your adventure now. Let's see how mentally clear, how inwardly still, and how authentic and transparent you can be. It will be of great benefit to those you have the good fortune to work with.

The more appropriately we honor our Energetic Weight, the greater we can individuate, or live according to who we really are. As Joseph Campbell said, "The privilege of a lifetime is finding out who you are." The greater the individuation, the less we crave belonging to things outside of us because we are truly confident and comfortable in who we are. The greater the individuation is, the greater the creational authority. This means we can create whatever we want without thinking, "We can't because we're not _____ [fill in the blank with "good enough," "smart enough," or something else]." The person with proper, sustained Energetic Weight earns proper individuation and has high creational authority.

To consistently "stand" in your Energetic Weight, it is necessary to do three things:

- Relinquish the ego's perpetual quest to control and/or seek approval.

- Understand which of your Organismic Rights (Chapter 4) is contributing to your "playing small" or not standing fully in your Energetic Weight.

- Assess your and your team's Leadership Levels (see PowerYourTribe .com), and map out a plan to increase them.

Understanding these three things and sharing this information with your key direct reports will enable you to invite them to stand in their true Energetic Weight.

Now sometimes we need to kick it up a notch. This is where clearing and recalling our energy makes all the difference.

Tool: Energy Recall

We all place energy out in the world—in people, places, projects, and elsewhere. We place energy generally in an attempt to get something accomplished (for example, we place energy in key colleagues to help them get a project done for us or our partners to get them to do what we want). We also place energy when we have a negative judgment about people— in that case, we'll push our energy out to them to try to make them change.

The trouble is we often leave our energy where we placed it even when its purpose is complete. Countless clients of ours have gone through this Energy Recall process only to find they still had energy in former coworkers from years ago!

Here's how it works:

1. Close your eyes. See a large golden sun about four feet above your head. This is your energy. Now, in your mind's eye, flick a switch and notice that the sun is now magnetic. Ask it to call back your energy from wherever you have placed it: in other people, physical locations, specific projects, maybe even in your calendar. Many people see the energy coming back in disks, like pancakes or Frisbees; others see it as streaming energy or light. See it however you see it.

2. Regardless of the form the energy takes, track where it came from. Where had you placed it? You can do this by "looking" at who is at the other end of the returning energy. If you see energy as a disk, flip the recalled energy disk over. Can you see what is written on the back? Is it someone's name, or a location, or a project? See the energy stream or disk rejoining your sun and merging back into it.

3. When you understand how much energy you are putting out and to whom, you will understand why you sometimes feel drained. Then you can work on putting energy into the positive alternative, the Relationship Bubble, which is the third part in each relationship— the "us." With every relationship, something is being created, which is the merger of the two people, the joint "project." When you put

your energy there and not directly into the other person, you will not feel drained.

4. Once your energy is recalled, flip a switch on the sun and see the energy in the form of golden light pouring down into you and over you until you're solid golden light. Then see it radiating off you to your office, town, state, country, and the globe.

Visit www.PowerYourTribe.com for a video that will guide you through this process. This technique was taught to me in many variations by several teachers, including Myra Lewin (www.halepule.com) and others. I am grateful to them all.

Once you've gotten present to your Energetic Weight and are regularly increasing it by using tools such as the Energy Recall, you can up your game with Myelination Practice.

MYELINATION: HOW YOUR BRAIN GETS SMARTER

"What's your greatest fear?" I asked Bill Gates one night at a Thai restaurant as we slurped Tom Yum Gai.

"Easy—not getting smarter."

Bill then laid out his plan to ensure that he'd always be surrounded by super smart people.

Maybe he didn't know about myelin.

The Smarter Secret

Let's assume "smarter" means making better choices and getting more of what you want and less of what you don't. Let's assume "smarter" means learning things faster, having more aha moments, and breaking through mental barriers swiftly and with deep fulfillment. Myelination is how leaders rapidly shift behaviors, stay emotionally agile, maintain or increase their Energetic Weight, and help their teams to do the same.

Here's how it works.

Roughly half of your brain is made of gray matter (where neural pathways are forged and reside), and the other half is made of white matter. More on this in a moment. First, it's key to remember that neurons that fire together wire together. This means that to learn something new, to set a new habit in place, repetition is required. When you practice something deeply, intentionally, and with some element of struggle, a neural pathway is formed. Neurons are now firing together in a new sequence and thus are wiring together as a collective. Repeated firing signals that this neural pathway is important. Repeated firing with deep practice and either struggle or ecstasy alerts oligodendrocytes and astrocytes that this pathway needs to be upgraded, or insulated, and the process of myelination begins (Figure 9.2).

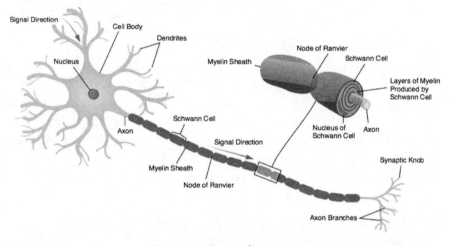

Figure 9.2 Myelination

The newly forged and repeatedly fired neural pathway is then insulated the way an electrical wire is wrapped in a protective coating. This pathway (gray matter) is strengthened via the myelin (white matter) insulation, and it is transformed from the equivalent of dial-up to broadband. Heavily myelinated neural pathways are up to 300 times faster—they've been optimized for speed and efficiency. They've also become the default behavior, as the brain will choose the most highly myelinated pathways (because clearly they are the most important). This is how we form new automatic behaviors, also known as "habits," or habitual behavior choices.

What Einstein Did

When Einstein's brain was autopsied in 1984, record amounts of myelin were found. Does it mean he was smarter than most? Not necessarily. Does it mean he persevered, failed, and kept learning and pushing forward with deep, focused practice? Yes.

I've been using this understanding of myelin and the myelination process with my executive coaching clients for the last few years. The results have been remarkable:

> **Anxiety removal:** The COO of a $500 million consumer packaged goods company did three neuro-coaching sessions over a period of six weeks. Then I gave her myelination homework. One month later she no longer suffered from debilitating anxiety. It's still absent six months later. This high-functioning CEO had suffered in silence for 47 years.

> **Managing emotions:** A senior partner at a Fortune 100 financial services firm regularly got triggered by backstabbing and political maneuvers when dealing with some difficult partners whom he couldn't avoid. He would get highly irritated, which affected his ability to be present and collaborative and to lead the team to the best outcome. We did four neuro-coaching sessions on this topic, plus myelination homework. He now navigates shark-infested waters with ease, diplomacy, and even a little humor.

> **Increased vision and innovation:** The head of an R&D lab was stuck. He hadn't had a good idea in ages, and the pressure was on, which only made matters worse. After three months of coaching and a few weeks of myelination practice, he designed three new products, with one already having preorders exceeding $100 million.

Now you know the secret: let's start myelinating.

Tool: Myelination Practice

To myelinate properly, you must do three things:

1. Try a new behavior and persevere through the uncomfortable part of learning and stretching. Think back to when you learned the Outcome Frame. You had to spend 15 minutes doing it. Fifteen! Bet it felt like a long time. When you wanted to gloss over uncomfortable questions (such as "What of value might you risk

or lose?"), you had to sit with them, dig deeper, and find an honest answer. It's like doing the full set of reps at the gym when your muscles are screaming or running the last mile in the race when you are exhausted.

2. Do this new behavior repeatedly in intense bursts (and short is OK). Repetition is key—myelin is living tissue: if you stop firing a pathway for 30 days, the myelin will start to break down. Did you play the piano as a kid? If it's been years since you've touched one and you try to play it, you'll know what I am talking about. If you make this new behavior a priority by setting timers in your calendar or having a note next to your bed and on your desk, you'll remember.

3. See, hear, and feel yourself doing the new behavior. Really get into it. Feel the good feelings and be totally in that desired state. Remember what Einstein said: "Imagination is everything—it is the preview of coming attractions." Remember how you stepped deeply into the future you envisioned in the Outcome Frame to "test drive" the possible outcome? Do the same here. Dive in, all the way.

Imagination results in firing; repeated firing results in myelination. Observing someone who is excellent at a behavior you want to acquire or grow also helps myelination.

Innovators and thought leaders refuse to be "socialized into reasonableness," into being told what is and isn't possible. Don't you cave in either!

Neuroscientists worldwide are increasingly studying myelin and its amazing impact on rapid learning, mastery, and neuroplasticity. So keep your circuits strong with deep, focused practice—myelination requires quality versus quantity. I ask clients to do the Myelination Practice I design for them for a minimum of 5 days in a row, five times per day, for only a few minutes each. For even better results, they do it for 10 days. What I find in coaching some of the top performers on the planet is that it is key to forge new—or turbocharge existing—pathways that are heavily insulated (myelinated) and that then become the default behavior pathways.

What new behaviors would you like? Find a neuroscience-based coach who uses myelination or design your own practice and get started. Now that you've got your own Energetic Weight stabilized, let's help others shift their behaviors with some useful and easy feedback tools.

GIVING AND RECEIVING FEEDBACK: HOW TO MAKE RAISING THE BAR FUN

Giving feedback is an art. And it's a necessary one because it helps us course-correct. And when done right, it promotes a culture of continuous improvement in which people don't perceive failure as such but rather as an opportunity to learn, adjust, and capitalize.

Proper feedback is also an advanced version of *consenting*, something we covered in Chapter 3. Rather than resisting what is happening, consenting is about *including* what's happening in your experience and making new choices. For example, if people have been ineffective in their role in sales, you don't want them to resist their poor performance for the month. You want to create a space where they can include their result (or lack thereof), take the learning from the experience, and improve. If they stay in resistance, no improvement is available.

With frequent and proper feedback, you can train your team and organization to *auto-course-correct*. When the team understands that they can take their own action, have their own consequences, and release resistance to those consequences (if they seem negative), they are on their way to being a Smart Tribe that *thrives* no matter how turbulent the times. They get stronger and stronger with the currents of change rather than shrinking from the challenges that come with them.

Proper and frequent feedback *is* power for your tribe.

Tool: Feedback Frame

Here's how to use the Feedback Frame for frequent, informal feedback. This tool has a very simple structure. There are only two statements:

- What worked or what's working is [list things here].

- What I'd like [or need*] to see more of is [list things here].

Note: The word "need" is used when you have given the same feedback previously and the person has not incorporated it. When the feedback is crucial, the word "need" can be used to create a stronger sense of urgency.

Make sure you have equal amounts of what worked or is working and what you'd like to see more of.

Also, make sure you encourage your team members to use this tool with you too—the Feedback Frame is most helpful when used up, down, and across the org chart. We all need feedback to learn and grow and connect with others and ourselves.

Tool: Four Conversations

Another method our clients like is the Four Conversations. The default stance here is to be curious, not angry or irritated. The Four Conversations are helpful to use when people have dropped accountability. Remember, be *curious*!

1. **Are you OK?** Always ask this the first time, as they may not be OK. A personal life challenge may have blindsided them, which is why they dropped the ball. If they are indeed OK, discuss the missed deadline, explain how accountability is essential at the organization so we can rely on one another, and help them with managing deadlines and time if necessary.

2. **Is there too much on your plate?** If a drop occurs again, check to see if there's too much on their plate. You likely piled on the work, and they are buried. It's time to prioritize. Have them make a list of their high-value and low-value activities and see what can be ditched, delegated, or deferred. See www.PowerYourTribe.com for a resource to help you.

3. **Is this role not the right fit for you?** The role may have become too big as your organization has grown. Find out if they have too many responsibilities or if the role just doesn't work anymore. If they say it does, use the Seven-Step Feedback Frame that follows.

4. **Do you really want to work here?** If you've had all the previous conversations and you've tried the Seven-Step Feedback Frame and you are still seeing accountability drop, you need to have a heart-to-heart. Their behavior is showing they aren't committed. It's probably time to say sayonara.

Tool: Seven-Step Feedback Frame

Now and then we need to pull an employee or colleague aside and talk about performance. Here's how to do it with respect and effectiveness, which keeps everyone in their Smart State. You can use this framework in any challenging situation, such as a conflict or misunderstanding, or a full counseling and turnaround scenario.

By the way, if you know a counseling and turnaround period is required, clarify the following issues *before* meeting with the employee or colleague:

- Determine what the counseling and turnaround period should be: 30, 60, or 90 days, depending on the complexity of the behavior change.

- Next, think through the specific behaviors you need changed, as well as what level of support you are willing to provide.

- Last, determine the consequences if the behavior does not change (demotion? termination?) or if the behavior does indeed change (keep current job? move to another team? get back on partner track?).

Good—now schedule the meeting with the employee or colleague who needs counseling and use the following Seven-Step Feedback Frame during the meeting.

Our clients love this process because it helps everyone get to a shared positive understanding for growth and resolution:

1. **Set the stage.** Explain why you're meeting and the outcome you want so that you can form a collaborative turnaround plan.

2. **State observable data and behavior.** Here you describe specific behaviors that must change and provide examples so that the employee can "step into" the past scenarios.

3. **Describe impact.** Describe the damage that these behaviors are doing to others, the company, and the employee himself or herself.

4. **Check problem acknowledgment.** Do they agree that there is a problem? Do they agree this problem now must end? This is the most essential step. If you don't reach agreement here, go back to step 1. Once agreement is reached, you'll notice that steps 5 through 7 are more pleasant because the employee will now be engaged in finding a solution.

5. **Create a plan together.** Set a time period (30 to 90 days) in which you'll meet weekly for 15 to 30 minutes to track their progress on releasing the challenging behaviors identified. Make the plan very specific in terms of what you need to see and when you'll know you got the outcome you wanted. If the turnaround doesn't occur, state clearly what the consequences will be (lost job, for example).

6. **Check understanding.** Is everything clear? Anything else you need to cover? Reiterate the desire for a positive resolution so the consequences can become irrelevant.

7. **Build small agreements.** Launch the plan and commit to ending the conflict once and for all. Be sure to track it frequently and make sure all concerned see the behavior change too. Some of our clients like to have the employees sign off on the above to ensure that this information gets in the talent and HR files (and the employees take this change effort seriously).

Here are some examples.

Patty's Plan

Patty was an executive at an insurance company we worked with many years ago. She regularly showed up late to both internal and external meetings, played on her mobile phone or doodled during meetings, often interrupted the CEO in meetings, and got defensive when people tried to give her respectful feedback. She was also a bit of a loner and didn't play well with others when collaboration was required. The CEO was finally ready for a Seven-Step Feedback Frame after she interrupted him repeatedly to "clarify" his points during an investor meeting.

What needs to change:

1. Show up on time to all meetings, phone calls, and appointments.

2. Be fully present and pay attention.

3. No interrupting: be respectful and understand your role.

4. No defending: collaborate, work with others.

If rapid change doesn't occur within the first 30 days, her role will be changed to a nonexecutive role and her compensation will be reduced.

How we'll monitor it:

Over this 30-day plan, weekly progress reports were due each Sunday by midnight (or sooner), stating progress in all four areas and what specifically Patty had changed or what she was implementing to make change permanent. Leadership also checked in with Patty's colleagues to ensure that they experienced the change too.

These terms were provided in written format so that Patty understood what was needed and what was at stake.

This format enabled Patty to finally "get" that she had to change these behaviors—or get a new job. She hunkered down, and we coached her through the root issues that caused these behaviors, and we also helped her build a stronger connection and rapport with her colleagues. Her behavior changed, and she got to keep her job.

Max's Plan

Max was a graphic artist at an advertising agency. Although deeply gifted as a designer and an artist, he had some challenging behaviors. He often shut down or ignored people who had points of view different from his (note this cognitive bias from Chapter 8). Also, the organization had an overall cultural challenge of people talking over one another, and Max was the leader in this behavior. He often made decisions based on what benefited him, not the team, and he didn't look out for others very often.

What needs to change:

1. Listen to and consider other points of view.

2. One person speaks at a time—**no** interrupting. If unclear, ask if the person is done talking.

3. We're a unified front with a unified goal. We always have each other's back. Period.

How we'll measure it:
Weekly monitoring and discussion.

How we'll know when we have it:

1. Max's actions will put the company's interests first and not his own, and he'll be less concerned with title, position, and reporting structure.

2. Peers will no longer complain about his interrupting them.

3. Max will talk less and listen more.

We coached him for an intense 90 days to turn around his key challenging behaviors. He was a quick study, and he was super receptive to coaching, so we made great progress. Then his leader invested more deeply in Max due to his desire to grow and change. Now Max leads the entire design department, and we've had the pleasure of coaching him through two key revenue inflection points.

HOW DO YOU HANDLE FEEDBACK?

Here's a feedback check-in for you:

- How skilled is your team at giving formal feedback?

- Does your tribe feel comfortable giving and receiving frequent and open feedback (both positive and negative)?

- How are accountability misses handled? Are responsibilities transparent?

SUMMARY

1. Energetic Weight is made up of the energy, power, and authority that come with a given role. It is about owning the appropriate amount of

authority and responsibility that comes with your role. When we are in proper Energetic Weight, things flow. When we are not, there is chaos.

2. We all place energy out in the world—in people, places, projects, and elsewhere—to get something accomplished. The trouble is that we often leave our energy where we placed it even when its purpose is complete. The Energy Recall process helps us recall energy that we may have left "out there" with coworkers from years ago!

3. Heavily myelinated neural pathways are up to 300 times faster— they've been optimized for speed and efficiency. They also become the default behavior, as the brain will choose the most highly myelinated pathways. Increasing myelination with practice helps us become more agile.

4. Giving proper feedback is necessary. The more we practice and encourage useful behaviors, the more automated they become. With frequent and proper feedback, you can train your team and organization to auto-course-correct.

5. When your team understands that they can take their own action, have their own consequences, and release resistance to those consequences, they are on their way to being a Smart Tribe that *thrives* no matter how turbulent the times.

TWITTER TAKEAWAYS

-   Energetic Weight, or how we "show up," is essential to building healthy teams and companies.

-   If you don't stand in your Energetic Weight, someone else will, or if you're the leader, anarchy will result.

-   Too many leaders, in an attempt to "be nice," to fit in, or to be popular, miss the opportunity to stand in their Energetic Weight.

-   Giving feedback is an art. And it's a necessary one because it helps us course-correct.

RESOURCES

See this chapter's section on www.PowerYourTribe.com for the following:

- Chapter *Quick Take* video

- Leadership Level Resource: Let your team self-assess their level and then discuss how to raise it.

- *Energy Recall* video

- Leadership Lunch Process: Peer-Based Coaching via a Book Club Format

PART **III**

THE *POWER YOUR TRIBE* PLAYBOOK CASE STUDIES

Resilience Rx: Leadership Abusing Power and Engaging in Bullying Behavior

The VP of finance at a media company constantly interrupts and actively prevents others from speaking in meetings. He scoffs when they share ideas or make suggestions.

A managing director at a financial services firm publicly trashes another director's new strategy, tearing it apart without having the domain expertise to truly understand what she is saying.

The lead software engineer makes snide remarks about the product development process during team meetings. He publicly denounces the marketing team too.

What do these all have in common? They are leaders abusing power, even bullying. Bullies are far too often tolerated in the workplace. Why? Because people don't want to be attacked and dragged into the conflict. Because the bully is a star performer or rainmaker. And sometimes because it is easier to simply do nothing.

A shocking 75 percent of U.S. workers are affected by bullying,[1] so it's essential to tackle this tough topic here.

ASSESS: WHAT WE FOUND

In all the situations in which leadership was abusing power that we have been called into, we have needed to address three key challenges, described below.

1. Identify How the Bullies Have Been Allowed to Thrive

Paul, the COO, was managing the VP of finance bully mentioned earlier. During coaching, Paul realized how he was tolerating, and even allowing, this unacceptable behavior.

Here's how Paul was enabling the bully:

- He was allowing inappropriate conduct to occur in meetings instead of stopping the bully from constantly interrupting and preventing others from speaking. Paul needed to clarify what appropriate meeting etiquette was and ensure that it was being honored.

- He was acting as a go-between whenever the bully refused to interact with people he thought were "stupid" instead of making it clear to both parties that they needed to work things out together.

- He was suppressing his anger and thus compromising his integrity instead of dealing with this issue directly. Instead, he needed to model leadership for his team and provide a safe, respectful, and collaborative work environment.

- He was letting others vent to him about the bully instead of creating an opportunity to let disgruntled parties communicate their grievances directly and interface with HR.

We all avoid uncomfortable human relations issues sometimes. But the cost of doing that is exorbitant as we daily give our power away, compromise our integrity, and inadvertently teach our team that bullying is acceptable. This strips our team of emotional agility.

2. Uncover the Surprising Truth About What Bullies Wanted

Like all human beings, bullies crave safety, belonging, and mattering. Often one of these is exactly what the bully wants. They are just trying to get it in an ineffective and inappropriate way. Guess what each of these bullies wants:

- Person X puts others down, makes them feel small, and condescends because inside, person X doesn't feel he _____.

- Person Y spreads fear, rumors, and negative gossip because inside, person Y doesn't feel _____.

- Person Z talks about inequality, unfairness, and how others get special treatment because inside, person Z feels that she doesn't _____.

The answers are "matters," "safe," and "belong," respectively. Once you uncover what bullies want, you can start to give it to them. Give bullies what they crave as long as it furthers the behavior change you need. For example, you may need to give them some mattering to create the belonging you want—and note that you are going to tell the truth; you're not buttering them up to manipulate them.

Example: "I need your help. You're a great idea generator and natural leader, so I thought of you to help with the following. We have a terrific opportunity to strengthen the connection within our team in order to pull together to achieve our quarterly goals. Let's brainstorm next Tuesday, as this could be an initiative you could lead for us."

3. Determine Whether We Were Dealing with Borderline Behavior

By using the Borderline Behavior Quiz and Borderline Behavior Decoder from Chapter 8, our clients have been able to easily assess the kind of behavior they were dealing with. If it was a borderline behavior, they have been able to use the strategies in Chapter 8 to navigate these challenging types.

It's essential to note that borderline behavior is a common element in bullying, and true borderline behavior can only be *managed* with safety, belonging, or mattering, not *cured*.

ACT: WHAT WE DID

Our clients found that the Outcome Frame (Chapter 6), the Seven-Step Feedback Frame (Chapter 9), and the Borderline Behavior Quiz and Borderline Behavior Decoder (Chapter 8) were very helpful to them in working with difficult personalities.

We also recommended sharing these tools with their teams because all relationship breakdowns involve multiple participants. Destructive behavior rarely occurs in a vacuum. We used all these tools with Paul's team, for example. Then we helped Paul develop his *Three-Step Bully Rehab Plan*, described below.

1. Identify How You Are Enabling the Behavior

Paul was contributing to and playing a role in this dysfunction by allowing inappropriate conduct in meetings, acting as a go-between when the bully refused to interact with others, and suppressing his anger and thus compromising his integrity as a leader.

2. End the Enabling System

In the Tension Triangle of relationships, there are three key roles: the Persecutor, the Victim, and the Rescuer.[2] The bully is generally playing the Persecutor, which creates the need for a Rescuer to protect the Victim.

First, Paul helped the bully identify his persecuting behavior by using the Tension Chart (Table 10.1). Once this sank in, the bully was shown the Empowerment Chart (Table 10.2) so that he could see how the Persecutor could shift to the positive alternative of an Action Creator (Figure 10.1).

TABLE 10.1 Tension Chart

Victim	Rescuer	Persecutor
Thinks	**Thinks**	**Thinks**
• "I am powerless." • "I am at the mercy of unseen forces."	• "I must save the victim from perceived harm." • "If I don't help, no one else will."	• "I must win at any cost." • "No one follows through (or measures up or cares)."
Acts	**Acts**	**Acts**
• Focuses on problems • Relinquishes responsibility for actions	• Fosters dependency by becoming indispensable • Intervenes on behalf of the victim to shield him or her from harm	• Dominates others through criticism • Takes a command-and-control stance
Says	**Says**	**Says**
• "Why did you do that to me?" • "It's not my fault." • "There's nothing I can do." • "She (or he) told me to do it."	• "I'll make it better for you." • "I feel sorry for you." • "Let me help you." • "I'll do it so you won't have to."	• "Can't you do anything right?" • "What's wrong with you?" • "It's your fault."
Feels	**Feels**	**Feels**
• Mistreated • Hopeless • Discounted	• Fear of being abandoned • A sense of martyrdom when the victim doesn't accept advice or help • A need to be needed and a compulsion to protect or fix	• Discounted, and must ensure his or her power • Others are trying to thwart his or her desires • Out of control; lashes out to protect himself or herself • Perpetual disappointment in others

Source: With gratitude to Stephen Karpman and David Emerald for their work on triangle roles and empowerment.

TABLE 10.2 Empowerment Chart

Outcome Creator	Insight Creator	Action Creator
Thinks	**Thinks**	**Thinks**
• "I am powerful." • "I am energized." • "I am capable."	• "I am resourceful and creative." • "Other people are resourceful and creative."	• "All of life's lessons are opportunities for growth." • "Every person has great potential."
Acts	**Acts**	**Acts**
• Seeks help when needed • Takes action to achieve desired outcomes • Takes responsibility for actions and beliefs	• Cultivates hope in others • Uses inquiry to help others gain clarity about their desired outcomes and the actions to achieve them	• Focuses on improvement and development • Provokes the person to make choices and take action
Says	**Says**	**Says**
• "The outcome I want is ..." • "I own that behavior." • "I'm committed to making this happen." • "This is what I've learned."	• "What outcome would you like?" • "What will having that do for you?" • "When will you know you have it?" • "What are your next steps?"	• "You have a choice." • "What are you going to do?" • "What are you committed to?" • "You aren't doing what you said you would do." • "What are you willing to do about it?"
Feels	**Feels**	**Feels**
• Open to possibilities • Resourceful • Confident • Hopeful and optimistic	• Compassionate and caring toward others • Called to serve by helping people define what's important to them and to see new possibilities	• Confident and empowered to hold high standards • Compelled to provide a push toward action, acquiring new insights and knowledge • Compassionate yet may appear confrontational to others

Source: With gratitude to Stephen Karpman and David Emerald for their work on triangle roles and empowerment.

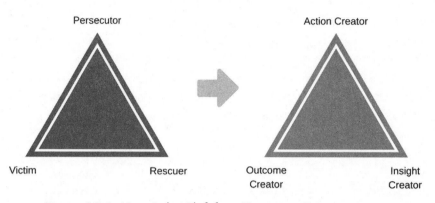

Figure 10.1 How Roles Shift from Tension to Empowerment

3. Set up a New System with Healthy Boundaries and Behaviors

Next, we had Paul pave the way for the Persecutor to shift to an Action Creator by using an Outcome Frame. Paul asked the bully the following questions:

1. "What would you like?" (The outcome the bully desires that he can create and maintain.)

2. "What will having that do for you?" (How the bully will feel and the benefits he will get.)

3. "How will you know when you have it?" (Proof or criteria that will be present.)

4. "Where, when, and with whom do you want this?" (Timing, who else, and scope.)

5. "What of value might you risk or lose to get this? What side effects may occur?" (Is it OK for the bully to have this outcome?)

6. "What are your next steps?"

By asking question 2 a few times, Paul was able to get to the bottom of what emotional experience the bully wanted. Considering the issues in question 2 often reveals what a bully really wants. The Outcome Frame is a potent tool to get a person to focus on the outcome and not the problem— it helps him or her get unstuck. Question 5 helps a great deal too.

Finally, Paul used a Seven-Step Feedback Frame (Chapter 9) to co-create a turnaround plan for the bully with regular check-ins to ensure that his behavior was changing.

Note that if the bully is above you on the organizational chart, you'll need talent (also called "human resources") or a mentor equal to or greater in stature than the bully to use this process successfully.

ROI: HOW THE ORGANIZATION BENEFITED

I'm thrilled to report that both Paul and his VP of finance have been transformed.

Paul has shifted from Rescuer to Insight Creator. If the VP of finance or any staff member comes to him to solve a problem, he calls a group meeting at which he lets them work it out.

The VP of finance now lets others speak in meetings and actively seeks their input. He has even implemented our Effective Meeting Process (see www.PowerYourTribe.com). He checks in with Paul, his peers, and his direct reports monthly, using a Feedback Frame to ensure that everyone is communicating clearly and feels respected.

Over the course of six months as we supported this turnaround, the ROI for Paul's company was the following:

- Finance team morale increased by 51 percent (this and the figures below below were measured by using the SBM Index), and the team members now walk tall, laugh, and joke around.

- Safety increased by 65 percent.

- Belonging increased 37 percent.

- Mattering increased by 44 percent.

- The team is even planning a birthday lunch for the VP of finance!

SUMMARY

1. Bullies want safety, belonging, and mattering too. However, their means of attaining them are often harmful, unworkable, and damaging to themselves and others.

2. We're all a little bit borderline—we all have tricky behavior at times. The key is to catch it, navigate it, survive, and ultimately thrive.

3. Every Victim needs a Persecutor, and every Persecutor needs a Victim. In between them is a Rescuer. We all have a role to play when it comes to bullying and difficult personalities.

4. The Outcome Frame is a great tool to redirect people's attention toward a solution rather than to the existing problem. It helps us step out of a problem-focused system.

TWITTER TAKEAWAYS

- We all avoid uncomfortable human relations issues sometimes. But at what cost? Exorbitant.

- Once you uncover what bullies want, you can start to give it to them. You can also help shift bullies from tension to empowerment.

- All relationship breakdowns involve multiple participants. Destructive behavior rarely occurs in a vacuum.

- Until we understand and adjust our communication, we can't increase trust, engagement, or influence.

RESOURCES

See this chapter's section on www.PowerYourTribe.com for the following:

- Effective Meeting Process: Learn how to reduce meetings and meeting times by up to 50 percent.

CHAPTER 11

Resilience Rx: Sluggish Sales and Competitive Crush

ompetitive crush is a term we use when a new (or sometimes existing) competitor has surged powerfully into the marketplace. For the business under threat, it feels like the competitor swooped out of left field. It sees the competitor raiding its top performers and key customers like an unstoppable force of nature.

In this instance, our client hadn't anticipated the potential threat, and it crushed their confidence. Salespeople were disheartened and discouraged, and market share eroded overnight. It was a total threat to survival, and everyone was in Critter State.

ASSESS: WHAT WE FOUND

Competitive crush was showing up for this specific organization in three key ways:

1. **Sales eroding:** Within two quarters, 15 percent of one product line and 37 percent of the other had been taken by the competitor. The competitor was eating our client's proverbial lunch.

2. **Staff exodus:** By the time we were called in, our client had lost three of its top salespeople—who had historically brought in 67 percent of its top-line revenue—to its competitor, who had offered

compelling salary and commission structures that our client simply could not match.

3. **PR problems:** Even though it wasn't true, the competitor's PR bluntly stated that our client's products were outdated and risky to use. The negative perception was so powerful that even our client's employees started to question our client's products, further increasing staff attrition.

This situation was a basic psych out. But we knew we could turn it around. We needed intense and immediate efforts to shift perception via powerful messaging both inside the organization to the team and outside the organization to the clients, prospects, and the marketplace overall. We had to first stop the sales losses, start an upswing, and keep staff in place.

The CEO was already on board. We met with the executive team. They were ready to make new meaning, but they didn't know how yet. But once that was done, we would establish an updated identity, enroll and engage the client-facing team members first and then the organization overall, and continue to expand the identity of tribe members and increase agility over time (see Figure 11.1).

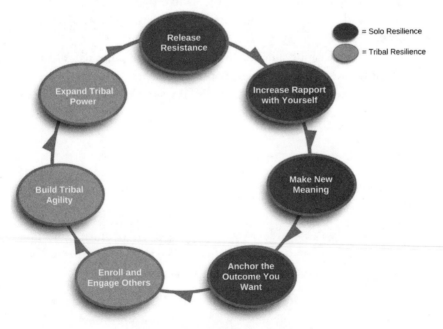

Figure 11.1 The Resilience Cycle

ACT: WHAT WE DID

First, we held a two-day offsite where we taught the most essential tools from our Neuroscience of Optimal Teams and Neuroscience of Navigating Change trainings. For this client situation, we focused on the Emotion Wheel (Chapter 3), Maneuvers of Consciousness (Chapter 3), Reframing (Chapter 5), Distorted Thinking Decoder (Chapter 5), Neuro Storytelling (Chapter 5), SBM Index (Chapter 7), SBM Communication (Chapter 7), and Meta Programs (Chapter 7) tools.

Then we created three sprint teams of three to five cross-functional leaders per team. The first team would stop the eroding sales and start gaining back market share, the second would stop salesperson attrition and ensure that we retained the team, and the third team would work on the perception challenge.

Team 1. Securing Sales

We held a one-day Sales and Marketing Intensive to map out our plan first to secure sales and then to develop programs to boost sales once the bleeding had stopped. To prepare for this, we asked the following questions:

- What percentage of your salespeople are performing at quota?

- How many stages are in the sales process? Can you please tell us what happens at each stage? At which stages do sales get stuck and/or slow down?

- What's your current sales cycle? What would you like it to be, and by when?

- What percentage of your pipeline do you close? What percentage would you like, and by when?

- What percentage of sales do you lose to competitors? What are the most common reasons? What percentage would you be willing to tolerate, and by when?

- What are your customers' and prospects' five greatest pain points?

- What's your current client retention rate? What would you like it to be, and by when?

- What are your current margins? What would you like them to be, and by when?

- How many qualified leads are generated each month? Through what channels? How many would you like, and by when?

- What marketing channels are you currently using (for example, trade shows, social media, webinars, infographics, blogs, and ads)? Which are the most effective?

We then sketched out the Safety, Belonging, and Mattering (SBM) Triggers and Meta Program (MP) Profiles (see Chapter 7) of the most at-risk customer categories. Later we'd get to all of them, as well as complete Customer Journeys. After this, we listed all the top influencers we'd need to get on board (or back on board). Finally, we launched our counterattack.

Team 2. Retaining Talent

Sometimes people will quit before they ask for what they want or tell you what is wrong. That's why knowing what to look for is so powerful.

The organization needed to rapidly ramp up engagement, communication, and trust. So we did an SBM Index as described in Chapter 7, and then we created and launched the key cultural programs: stronger and more compelling mission, vision, and values statements, Individual Development Plans, Leadership Lunches, Weekly Wins, Accountability Structures, Rock Star of the Month, Performance Self-Evaluations, Feedback Frames, and Impact Descriptions. We did a six-month culture coaching engagement to create and launch these programs, using our *SmartTribes Playbook* templates to expedite the results (see www.SmartTribesInstitute .com/STP).

Team 2 immediately assessed all key players by working with the Talent Team to identify the following "exit indicators":

1. **Productivity and accountability drop.** These team members are missing deadlines, are not achieving needle movers, and aren't keeping normal hours, or if they are in the office, they aren't fully present. They have stopped making commitments to long-term projects, and they aren't offering forward-thinking ideas. They don't

seem to care or want to step up, grow, stretch, or course-correct. These once top producers are now *not* producing.

2. **Communication stops.** They aren't proactively contributing in meetings, aren't responding to e-mails or phone calls in a timely manner, or sometimes don't respond at all. They are isolating themselves, and they are doing only the minimum in keeping the lines of communication open and constructive. When asked if everything is OK, they get defensive or fake it.

3. **Negative attitudes and behaviors appear.** They are expressing negative opinions about work, aren't satisfied, and have nothing positive to say, and they aren't optimistic, outcome focused, or proactive. They play the blame game, and they may even display bullying behavior.

4. **Changes in appearance become evident.** Drastic changes in appearance, combined with changes in behavior, can indicate that team members aren't interested in how they are perceived at work or that they don't feel they are "seen" at work, so how they dress or appear doesn't really matter.

5. **Team members are concerned.** When team members express their concerns, it's a sign something is serious. Since team members work closely together, they will be the first to notice subtle changes. It's important to ensure that these concerns don't become office gossip, so at this point, take a moment to check in with the top producer.

Once our clients saw these behaviors, they acted to turn the experience around and reengage the team member. To help them do this, we used our brain-based executive coaching techniques.

For example, our Seven-Step Feedback Frame (Chapter 9) was a helpful process in bringing the disengaged or challenging employee back on board. Our client also found it powerful to check in with a "flight-risk employee" *before* that team member checked out.

If you are working in a situation like this, you'll want to use our brain-based techniques to help all involved get to a shared positive understanding. It's OK to start with your concerns that a team member is drifting away based on whichever of the exit indicator behaviors are relevant. And it's essential to come from a caring, listening place, first finding out if the person wants to stay and then forging a go-forward plan together. Remember, it's about creating more safety, belonging, and mattering.

In our work with this client in the midst of a competitive crush, we invited all team members to be in a Leadership Lunch group (see www .PowerYourTribe.com). In addition, the potential flight risks as well as the highest potential associates were offered an opportunity to apply to participate in a Leadership Development Program.

Team 3. Perception Turnaround

Here we used a three-pronged approach: calls from key executives to all clients, a potent content strategy to raise the organization's profile and position it more powerfully as a thought leader, and an influencer campaign to ensure that those who influenced the clients and prospects most powerfully were on board.

The tools we used in all three strategies were Neuro Storytelling, Meta Programs, and SBM Communication.

ROI: HOW THE ORGANIZATION BENEFITED

The Sales, Talent, and Perception Teams all did exceptional jobs. Here are the fruits of their labors:

- **Recovered and strengthened sales:** Our client won back the market share that had been lost, recovering 100 percent of the lost customers on the first product line and 89 percent on the second product line. The entire process took almost two years because, frankly, product changes had to occur and not all the perceptions the competitor had created were false. The great news was that thanks to product enhancements, our client created new products that started crushing those of the competitor. Game on!

- **Increased staff retention:** Our client retained 97 percent of the salespeople, all the marketing people, all the high potentials, and key staff. A few associates left due to retirement or relocation for a spouse's career.

- **Boosted employee engagement:** The SBM Index showed us engagement was at 65 percent when we started. Over the next 12 months, the Talent Team moved engagement by an impressive 13 points to 78 percent.

The best part was the new spring in everyone's step, the heads held high, the improved camaraderie, and the shouts of enthusiasm in the sales and marketing area when the horn was blown as each customer was won back.

SUMMARY

1. Change is power for your tribe. When our client came to us, the organization's entire existence was threatened. After working with the resilience tools, the organization recovered sales, retained key staff, dramatically improved one product line, and boosted employee engagement.

2. The SBM Index gives us a clear picture of where more safety, belonging, and mattering are needed in the organization. The cultural programs help fill the gaps so that teams can move from Critter State to Smart State.

3. Customers want more safety, belonging, and mattering too. When we combine this understanding with Meta Programs, we can launch campaigns to attain new clients and retain key client accounts.

4. Regular use of Feedback Frames is great for crisis response, course-correcting, *and* staff retention. It enables us to celebrate what team members are doing well, identify what they can do better, and identify what support is available to bring more safety, belonging, and mattering to their role.

5. Effective communication is key to altering people's perceptions, especially when it comes to PR. The main tools that help us achieve this include Neuro Storytelling, SBM Communication, and Meta Programs.

TWITTER TAKEAWAYS

- *Competitive crush* is a term we use when a new (or sometimes existing) competitor has surged powerfully into the marketplace, threatening an organization's success.

- Sometimes people will quit before they ask for what they want or tell you what is wrong. That's why knowing what to look for is so powerful.

- What percentage of your pipeline do you close? What percentage would you like, and by when?

- Check in with a flight-risk team member before that team member checks out.

- When you are bringing a disengaged employee back on board, it's all about creating more safety, belonging, and mattering.

RESOURCES

See this chapter's section on www.PowerYourTribe.com for the following:

- Leadership Lunch Process: Peer-Based Coaching via a Book Club Format

- See www.SmartTribesInstitute.com for info on our workshops, Sales and Marketing Intensive, Leadership Development Program, and more referenced in this chapter.

- *SmartTribes Playbook:* www.SmartTribesInstitute.com/STP

CHAPTER 12

Resilience Rx: Merger and Acquisition Adventures

O ur client had acquired three competitors, tripled their headcount, and quintupled their revenue in a four-year period. Revenue had surged from $50 million to $250 million as they moved rapidly through two key inflection points (each inflection point resulted in essentially an entirely new company).

Though mergers and acquisitions (M&A) are an exciting and powerful path to rapid growth, they often bring tremendous stress, leading to Critter State behavior.

ASSESS: WHAT WE FOUND

The amount of change from the acquisitions had hurt employee retention due to three competing cultures. One culture was very conservative (ties every day in every role), one culture was very laid back (jeans, flip-flops, T-shirts), and one culture was middle of the road, like the parent company.

Since the cultures hadn't been integrated into a single cohesive one, silos had formed, slowing effective information flow and decision-making. And trust was low as a result. Now that the basic integration was done, it was essential to ask, "Who are we going to be together? What is our tribal identity?" It was time to create trust and tribe.

Lack of trust creates an environment where concerns quickly evolve into fears. And when fears collide with a belief that the system is failing or that one doesn't and never will belong, trouble results. As distrust and fear increase, the negative impact on employee morale, engagement, and performance accelerates. The end results are disengaged employees, frustrated management, and lower profits. And the problem comes from four key emotional experiences:

1. **A sense of injustice:** The experience of unfairness tamps down the insula, the part of the brain responsible for emotional hurt and intuition. If a person is experiencing unfairness, he or she will spend more time in Critter State, which will adversely affect performance, decision-making, collaboration, and overall peace and happiness.

2. **Lack of hope:** The experience of hopelessness is even more painful than unfairness, and it's below the Critter State on the emotional range. In neurolinguistics, the states of hopelessness, helplessness, worthlessness, and grief or terror are considered Baseline States. It doesn't get more painful than this.

3. **Lack of confidence:** Depending on the person and the degree of lack of confidence, we'll likely see procrastination, reluctance to take risks, "playing small," and yes, more Critter State.

4. **Desire for change:** The desire for change is encouraging because it means there's some energy here. Desire for change means we can envision a possible future where things are better. This lights up the ventral striatum, where we anticipate reward. If we can increase this experience, we can get into Smart State.

ACT: WHAT WE DID

In this case, we had to release resistance (Chapter 3), make new meaning, establish a new identity (Chapter 5), and enroll and engage (Chapter 7).

First, we did an SBM Index (Chapter 7) to gauge how everyone felt and determine what they needed most. We found that people really wanted belonging (no surprise), and we did culture coaching for a year to create the cultural rituals to help people come together.

The new leadership team then did a roadshow to all sites to make people feel that "everyone is in it together" and to make clear that no single site was better than others. The main communication: "You are safe here, we are all in this together, and everybody matters."

We also had to acknowledge the grieving. After all, some well-loved employees had lost their jobs. You can't have two HR departments and two finance divisions. Some product lines and service offerings were cut as well because they weren't profitable or relevant to the new entity. So we designed parting rituals to process the grieving and to acknowledge and appreciate the parting people's contributions.

In parallel, we held a two-day leadership retreat to bring the leaders of the four companies together. Everyone took our Leadership Assessment (www.SmartTribesInstitute.com/lead) in advance so we could identify the Present State of the leadership team as well as what their top challenges were. We continued these retreats over the next three years as the organization continued to expand and acquire. We looped in the next level of leadership and held our four standard neuroscience trainings: leadership, influence, optimum teams, and navigating change. And we did a leadership development program for the highest potential leaders so we'd be ready when our client acquired the next few companies in their sights.

Together we forged a new vision and set of company values (and a new dress code: business casual). Here's the difference between mission, vision, and values:

- A *mission* is a long-term proposition that doesn't change. It answers the questions, "Why are we here as an organization?" "Why do we exist?" "What are we going to make happen because we exist?"

- A *vision* is aspirational—that is, it's a picture of what you want as an organization or as an individual, as far out on the horizon as you can see. Your vision can be three to five years into the future or even longer. What's the clear future you see for the organization? What do you want your world to be like, or what do you want to have achieved in the future?

- *Values* are what you honor and believe in, which will govern how you will behave as you fulfill your mission and create your vision. Values determine standards of behavior—that is, the code of conduct that you will not compromise.

We also made sure to set up diverse cross-functional teams for all new initiatives: cultural, sales, marketing, and operational. In a nutshell, we created more collaboration, communication, transparency, and mutual respect. Everyone owned the shared responsibility of rebuilding trust. *They were in it together.*

Because building sustainable trust was key, it meant taking employee engagement and empowerment to a new level, and it meant ensuring that leadership was engaged and empowered too. Engagement and motivation happen when people solve their own problems and create their own aspirations and expectations. That's why boosting communication via the Outcome Frame (Chapter 6) and the Feedback Frame (Chapter 9) is so powerful. Additionally, it was essential to do the following:

- Use inquiry over advocacy. Ask questions rather than give orders and use the Outcome Frame for deep insight and clarity creation.

- Hold team strategy and problem-solving meetings at every level. Meet to do the work, not to talk about the work (see PowerYourTribe .com for a valuable communication and meeting types resource).

- Have team members create their own goals and action plans.

- Add empowerment to engagement. When we did this, we witnessed even more profound results. The leaders learned that they could heal and prevent significant distrust by first understanding what a person was experiencing and then intentionally helping him or her shift into engagement and empowerment. The tools and methods we used included the Logical Levels of Change (Chapter 1); the Resilience Cycle (Part II); VAK Anchoring (Chapter 6); the SBM Behavior Decoder (Chapter 7); SBM Communication (Chapter 7); Meta Programs (Chapter 7); Organismic Rights (Chapter 4); Energetic Weight (Chapter 9); Myelination (Chapter 9); Neuro Storytelling (Chapter 5); Reframing (Chapter 5); and the Distorted Thinking Decoder (Chapter 5).

When we give people what they crave (more safety, belonging, and mattering), their critter brains calm down, and we can guide them into their Smart State.

ROI: HOW THE ORGANIZATION BENEFITED

Within the first year of working together, the organization improved from *85 percent retention to 90 percent*. Starting in the second year to date, the organization enjoyed 95 percent retention. People loved working there!

Our client successfully navigated the "people" work they had overlooked while zooming through two inflection points. That was all put in place during our first year together. Over the next three years, our client's growth surged from $250 million to *$400 million*.

The best part is, when you walk through the organization now, you see leaderboards tracking results, feel the enthusiasm and connection among this ever-expanding tribe, and hear people saying encouraging upbeat messages; they collaborate, joke with one another, and pat one another on the back.

SUMMARY

1. Growth can be threatening. Although profits and company size may increase, it can induce great internal stresses, putting safety, belonging, and mattering at risk.

2. When a company moves through an inflection point, it is effectively a new company, and its DNA must be redefined and reformed from the inside out.

3. The Resilience Cycle shows us how we can build solo resilience *and* tribal resilience so that the individuals' needs and the tribe's needs are met.

4. When key staff are lost, grieving occurs. This must be consented to, included, and catered to—otherwise it manifests as resistance to change.

5. To influence a company to create a better future, everyone's contributions (past and present) must be properly included and appreciated.

TWITTER TAKEAWAYS

- A lack of trust creates an environment where concerns quickly evolve into fears.

- When fears collide with a belief that the system is failing or that one doesn't and never will belong, trouble results.

- Having a desire for change means we can envision a possible future where things are better.

- Engagement and motivation happen when people solve their own problems and when they create their own aspirations and expectations.

- Use inquiry over advocacy: ask questions rather than give orders, and use the Outcome Frame for deep insight and clarity creation.

RESOURCES

See this chapter's section on www.PowerYourTribe.com for the following:

- Communication and Meeting Types Resource: Unpack and optimize how your team communicates.

- Revenue Inflection Point Chart: The Key Components to Ensure That Your Organization Moves to, and Through, Key Revenue Growth Milestones

- *Defining Personal Values* kit

CHAPTER 13

Resilience Rx: A Family Business and Board Dysfunction

n Chapter 9, we shared the Energetic Weight tool. You'll recall that Energetic Weight is like the foundation of a building. If one pillar is out of place, the entire structure is unstable.

The main challenges we see with family businesses all stem from people being out of their proper Energetic Weight. They include the following:

- *Nepotism,* when family members hold key roles for which they aren't qualified

- *Lack of diversity,* when only family members have key roles, and so no outside perspectives are brought in

- *Tunnel vision,* when key roles are held by people who have little or no experience in the business world overall outside the family's business

These challenges lead to significant biases, which can all be overcome to help the company thrive.

One client called us after the leaders had attended a day-long training we held with the Young Presidents' Organization. A transfer of power had occurred, and the new CEO wanted some new strategies to influence, enroll, and engage her board of *family members.*

She had compelling plans to lead the organization to the next level, yet the board wanted "business as usual." That might've been OK, except "usual" no longer was on the menu. The world, marketplace, and workforce had changed too much in the last 40 years to continue with "business as usual."

ASSESS: WHAT WE FOUND

The board was composed solely of family members, with nine board seats. Five board members had zero business experience. They had been enjoying six-digit dividends annually for over 25 years. We had to help them feel safe that their dividends would continue as we moved the company forward.

The next challenge? The "kids" were now in charge, yet the dad continued to meddle, micromanage, and even discuss confidential company business at his golf club. Dad wanted to matter still—yet he also wanted to be retired and free of the day-to-day responsibilities. We had to figure out a way for him to have both.

The CEO had been pressured to offer roles to some family members who were not truly qualified. Her cousin's 26-year-old son was pressed by the board into a position of power that he didn't know how to handle successfully.

The result? Smart people were making bad decisions, and the people who should have had power due to significant experience were shut out or their impact was minimized. It was time to turn this around.

ACT: WHAT WE DID

We started coaching the CEO immediately. Then, together with the CEO and the executive team, we forged a plan.

First, we held our Neuroscience of Influence training so that all the key players could navigate the family dynamics more powerfully. Then we held our Neuroscience of Leadership training, as many of the leaders had never learned about the key brain-based leadership tools. Next, during a two-day retreat together, we mapped out the next three years of the company's growth and infrastructure. We drafted the organizational chart that would get us what we needed—and we identified many skill gaps. We made impact descriptions for who we'd need to hire and when.

Resistance needed to be released and new meaning made (Chapters 3 and 5). The "kids" needed to increase their Organismic Rights (Chapter 4) to have needs and exist in front of their larger-than-life charismatic dad. To do this, they had to increase rapport with themselves via the Parts Process, stand in their Energetic Weight (Chapter 9), and set healthy boundaries. We handled this via coaching.

Now we were ready for the board! We created a message to increase safety, belonging, and mattering—to enroll the board in attending a retreat. All agreed. Then we sent a high-level information package to the board outlining what would happen at the upcoming board retreat and how they could contribute. The CEO kicked off the event with a board dinner to celebrate the legacy the board and prior company leaders had created, stressing how their impactful work had laid the foundation for the growth to come. Everyone ended the evening feeling good with the new meaning that had been made.

In the morning, the CEO and the executive team took turns covering the components of the three-year plan and what this plan would mean to the organization overall, noting that the dividends would be steady-state or slightly reduced for a time. Investments needed to be made in the business that would over time increase the dividends.

All executives were trained to speak in the Meta Programs (Chapter 7) of the board members, which was a blend of Away, Procedures, General-Specific, Reflective, Sameness, and Sameness with Exception.

Over the course of the day, the board members became more and more comfortable so that by the afternoon they were downright excited. Now it was time to talk about how they wanted to operate as a board going forward. The CEO showed sample board codes of conduct and led the board in forging their own.

In the past, decisions had often been based on past personal grievances and historical alliances—instead of being ROI based—because the organization was not accountable to any outsiders. Part of the preparation work for the board included background reading on cognitive bias[1] and a copy of *SmartTribes*.

Once the board was on track with the three-year plan, we launched the recruiting effort. And once we had the new sales lead on board, we held a Sales and Marketing Intensive.

ROI: HOW THE ORGANIZATION BENEFITED

The CEO and the executive team did such a great job with the board retreat that we could move forward swiftly. Outside talent was brought in for diversity and more seasoned management (to reduce nepotism). The SBM Index and Meta Programs reduced turbulence during this transition within family messaging, and the clear path, plan, and budget helped the board and family buy in.

The board received monthly updates for the first year, and then quarterly for the second year onward. Dad was given the title "chairman emeritus" so he could continue to bask in the success that the "kids" were creating.

The company enjoyed the greatest growth to date—20 percent compounded annual growth rate (CAGR)—after our first year working together. They promoted several "old timers" into mentoring roles so the "young bucks" could bring the wisdom of the past forward into the present.

We developed the first-ever structure for the sales force, so new salespeople could sell (in addition to family members' sales efforts), and we entered two new geographic markets in our second year with them. Sales are now on a continuous CAGR of over 25 percent, the family is aligned, the board is functional, and the executive team is diverse.

The e-mails the "kids" receive from Dad and the board celebrate the company's wins, and the kids even receive verbal praise now and then at board meetings. The board is smiling instead of scowling, and they are supporting the company's leadership efforts instead of micromanaging.

SUMMARY

1. A lot of family business dysfunction is due to people being out of their proper Energetic Weight.

2. Key to getting everybody back into their Energetic Weight is assigning the right roles to the right people with the right capabilities and experience.

3. In a family business, senior family members hold essential wisdom that can be passed on to the younger ones. Their contributions must be recognized with respect. Doing this also helps release resistance to required change.

4. Increasing Organismic Rights enables younger family members to grow effectively into the roles they want to be in and the roles where they will perform best.

TWITTER TAKEAWAYS

- The main challenges we see with family businesses all stem from people being out of their proper Energetic Weight.

- Energetic Weight is like the foundation of a building. If one pillar is out of place, the entire structure is unstable.

- Nepotism, lack of diversity, and tunnel vision all lead to significant biases that can be overcome to help the company thrive.

- When turning business challenges around, resistance needs to be released and new meaning made.

- Leaders must increase rapport with themselves, stand in their Energetic Weight, and set healthy boundaries.

RESOURCES

See this chapter's section on www.PowerYourTribe.com for the following:

- Diversity, Equity, and Inclusion Optimization
- *Assessing Your Team's Performance* kit
- *Increasing Accountability and Ensuring Goals Are Met* kit

CHAPTER 14

Summary: What to Do Next

Phew! What a journey we have been on together. You've learned about resistance and how to release it and shift your awareness in short order. You've increased rapport with yourself to become more agile, and you've discovered that the meaning of what happens to us is what we choose. You've learned how to anchor the outcomes you want to create so that you can expedite your Desired State.

Then with all this newfound agility and resilience, you've learned how to enroll and engage others to help them build their agility and resilience and grow more powerful as a tribe.

Be sure to visit www.PowerYourTribe.com for helpful videos (great for team lunch-and-learns), extra resources to expedite your results, webinars, and other tools and treats. Your journey to powering your tribe at a whole new level has just begun.

Here we grow!

Acknowledgments

For over 40 years I've had remarkable teachers in the world of human behavior, human connection, performance optimization, neuroscience, emotional intelligence, and more. Formal teachers and informal teachers, but teachers all.

This book is a gratitude offering to these teachers for the countless gifts I have received, some of which I have shared with you in this book. All taught me that life is one big collaboration. Humans with humans, humans with nature, humans with themselves. We all matter, we all play a role, we all have equal value.

This book is also a love letter to our humanity—to our hopes, our fears, our present, our past, our future. Humans are remarkable beings—our courage, our loyalty, our capacity to love, and ultimately our resilience. My greatest wish is that this book will help enhance your resilience—and that of your tribe. More emotional resilience leads to more understanding, more compassion, and more momentum toward our Desired State.

You wouldn't be benefiting from this book without the help of many generous and committed people. My amazing husband, Geoff Heron, who supports me with all my wild ideas and projects, my tribe of remarkable friends—including Michele Ikemire, Theresa Teuma, Bonnie Digrius, Laura Fenamore, Jnana Gowan, Tracie Troxler, Bonnie Knezo, Peg Videtta, and Paul Vela—who keep me on track. My mom, Nancy Comaford, taught me a lot about resilience. My late great stepson Spike, who in his brief life of 21 years was the ultimate example of natural emotional resilience . . . I am so grateful for him.

Our amazing tribe at STI, my editors, our preview readers, and clients all played essential roles. The awesome duo of Alexis Chapman and Tami

Spence ensured the credits, graphics, and details were accurate and gave invaluable feedback throughout the lengthy process. I can always count on them for insights and creativity and to question me when I am veering off track. To them, I am deeply grateful. Heather Loizos and Wesley Hudnall helped behind the scenes with key components and support. Janet Schieferdecker helped me focus on the hottest topics. Amanda Rooker is an author's dream—I won't write a book without her! She made profound contributions to the structure of the book, all five drafts of it, and edited every word to ensure that everything flowed and made sense. I can't gush enough about the heart Amanda pours into her work. Jon Low helped me clarify the first major draft and added more life and dimensionality to the case studies and metaphors we used.

Our generous preview readers Amber Caska, Bonnie Knezo, Christine Crandell, Christine Royal Schindewolf, Geoff Heron, and Teresa Rodriguez showed me where I was being vague and where I needed to pick up the pace. I know you are busy, and I deeply appreciate your investing the time.

My mentors who call me on my "stuff" include Jerry Jampolsky, Diane Cirincione, don Oscar Miro-Quesada, Carl Buchheit, Ray Nobriga, Erica Alessio, Mona Wind and the 37 hospice patients I have had the honor to support in their final days—teachers all. Thanks for sharing your wisdom and helping me to remember what matters. To have Marshall Goldsmith, a fellow executive coach I greatly admire, write the foreword to this book was a huge boon. Thanks to Marshall and his terrific second in command, Sarah McArthur.

Thanks to my agent, Jim Levine, of Levine Greenberg, who stretched me to communicate what the purpose of this book truly is. Casey Ebro, my champion at McGraw-Hill, understood the power of this book and ensured it came to be. Mauna Eichner, my final edit and packaging pro, walked me through the at-times painful process. Donya Dickerson and Chelsea Van der Gaag contributed too. Thanks to you all and the extended team behind the scenes.

To the brilliant neuroscientists and cognitive science researchers at UCLA, Carnegie Mellon, Columbia, NYU, Stanford, Harvard, and the NeuroLeadership Institute, thanks for providing the research to support our real-world results.

And last, to the thousands of people I've met in my travels and at my speeches and had the great good fortune to work with, especially our courageous and committed clients: you have made all this work worthwhile. Every day you remind me that our time on this gorgeous and mysterious planet is fleeting, and there's no time like now. So let's power our tribe.

Life = the people we meet + what we create together

Thanks to everyone for being in my life. I am so very lucky to know you!

Appendix: Additional Resources

Table A.1 is a quick reference chart to help you find the tools you need in a given leadership or cultural change scenario, as well as additional resources to support you on your journey.

TABLE A.1 *Power Your Tribe* Quick Reference Chart

Challenge	Tools and Location
How to decide whether an experience is "good" or "bad" and shift from Critter State to Smart State	Releasing resistance (Chapter 3); meaning making and Reframing (Chapter 5)
How to understand your experiences and why you're feeling what; understanding where and how change happens	Logical Levels of Change, VAK, beliefs, and identity tools (Chapter 1); Emotion Wheel (Chapter 3)
Decoding the emotional experience that you or another person needs	Safety, belonging, and mattering (SBM) (Chapter 2); SBM Index (Chapter 7); Organismic Rights (Chapter 4); SBM Behavior Decoder and SBM Communication Tools (Chapter 7)
How to envision and then create a path from your Present State (PS) to your Desired State (DS)	Emotion Wheel and Maneuvers of Consciousness (Chapter 3); Outcome Frame (Chapter 6); Tension and Empowerment charts (Chapter 10)
Determine why you or others keep repeating painful or destructive behaviors and how to change this	Organismic Rights Decoder (Chapter 4); Parts Process (Chapter 4)
How to transform self-sabotage into success	Parts Process (Chapter 4)
How to interrupt repetitive thought patterns and create new grooves of thinking	Mindfulness Practices: News Feed, Brain Dump (Chapter 4), and Myelination (Chapter 9)

Challenge	Tools and Location
Shift perceptions, including your perception of yourself, others, a situation, or people's perception of themselves or things outside of them	Reframing, Distorted Thinking Decoder, and Neuro Storytelling (Chapter 5)
Help your brain make new neural connections and add more choices to your behavioral menu	VAK Anchoring (Chapter 6); Myelination (Chapter 9)
Help yourself and others to focus on the outcomes you want versus the problems you have; help shift out of Critter State; help gain clarity on Desired State (DS)	Outcome Frame and VAK Anchoring (Chapter 6)
How to communicate with people in their specific language — especially helpful when wanting to connect with another in recruiting or interviewing, conflict resolution, creating alignment and engagement, increasing motivation or leadership, getting others out of Critter State, giving sensitive performance feedback, sales conversations, and marketing messaging	Communication tools and Meta Programs (Chapter 7)
How to create more diversity, equity, and inclusion in your organization	Bias Navigation tools (Chapter 8)
How to determine the cause and navigation strategy of the most challenging behaviors, including bullying, entitlement, and extreme victimization	Borderline Quiz and Borderline Behavior Decoder (Chapter 8)
How to create the structures to support a passionately engaged culture	Cultural GAME Plan (Chapter 8)
How to unpack your experience of power, increase your and others' Energetic Weight and help teams to do the same	Energetic Weight Quiz, Energy Recall, and Myelination Practice (Chapter 9)
How to offer respectful and impactful feedback that sticks and how to train your team and organization to course-correct automatically and increase accountability	Feedback Frame, Four Conversations, and Seven-Step Feedback Frame (Chapter 9)
How to use the tools presented in Parts I and II in other situations as demonstrated in additional client case studies	Chapters 10 to 13

POWER YOUR TRIBE EMOTIONAL RESILIENCE ASSESSMENT

How's your emotional resilience and agility? Find out in five minutes or less! Simply take our Emotional Agility Assessment on www.PowerYour Tribe.com.

THE ROI OF POWERING YOUR TRIBE

At the end of the day we're all building businesses, teams, results. Here are a few metrics that our clients find result from using the tools in this book. You may want to consider using these measurements as key performance indicators (KPIs) for certain roles in your organization. Note that some of the ROI below can occur in as little as 90 days, whereas some will take longer, depending on your initial baseline and how ambitious the change initiative is:

- Individuals become 35 to 50 percent more productive.

- Individuals are 67 to 100 percent more emotionally engaged, loyal, accountable, and ownership focused.

- Leaders gain 5 to 15 hours per week because their teams and employees are more self-directed.

- 86 percent of our clients report getting more done in less time due to the accountability techniques they learned.

- 100 percent of our clients report that they are able to apply our communication techniques and thinking styles both at home and at work, resulting in an increase in personal fulfillment.

- 100 percent of individuals using our influence tools increase their ability to significantly influence others and outcomes.

- SBM Index scores increase 15 to 45 percent.

- Employee retention increases over 90 percent.

- Profit per employee increases by over 22 percent.

- Time to recruit open positions decreases by over 50 percent.

- Marketing messages are over 300 percent more effective.

- Inbound marketing demand generation increases by over 400 percent.

- Revenues and profits increase up to 210 percent annually.

- Sales are closed up to 50 percent faster.

- New products and services are created up to 48 percent faster.

- Up to 44 percent more of the sales pipeline is harvested.

About STI's Services

SmartTribes Institute (STI) helps organizations navigate growth and change to create new highs in performance and emotional engagement. It provides neuroscience-based coaching, workshops, and consulting to this end.

- **Leadership or culture coaching:** Get even greater performance and boost engagement to new highs. You'll apply *Power Your Tribe* tools to your greatest people and business challenges to achieve the following:

  o Increased productivity by 35 to 50 percent

  o Increased emotional engagement, loyalty, accountability, and ownership focus by 67 to 100 percent

  o Gains to leaders of 5 to 15 hours per week because their teams and employees are more self-directed

  o Safety, Belonging, and Mattering (SBM) Index score increased by 15 to 45 percent

  o Employee retention increased by over 90 percent

  o Profit per employee increased by over 22 percent

  o Time to recruit open positions decreased by over 50 percent

- **Sales and Marketing Intensive:** One of our most popular programs, this "roll up your sleeves" working session is delivered in a one- to two-day format with coaching afterward for implementation support. You'll learn to use Meta Programs, Safety, Belonging, and Mattering (SBM) tools, and a handful of other *Power Your Tribe* tools to achieve the following:

○ Close sales up to 50 percent faster.

○ Harvest 44+ percent more of your pipeline.

○ Make marketing messages 300+ percent more effective.

○ Increase inbound marketing demand generation by 400+ percent.

○ Increase revenues and profits by up to 210+ percent annually.

• **Deep learning workshops:** Take your team to the next level in record time.

THE NEUROSCIENCE OF COMPELLING LEADERSHIP

What would the impact be if you could tap into more parts of your brain to increase innovation, creativity, emotional engagement, vision, and feelings of safety, belonging, and mattering? And what would the impact be if you could guide your entire company to this state too?

You would accomplish the following:

• Learn what all human beings crave at a primal and neurological level—and how to give it to them.

• Understand how the brain works in change, growth, and learning scenarios—and how to shift the brain into enthusiasm and innovation versus fear and resistance.

• Discover how we use our attention (or don't use it) and the 50 to 70 percent emotional impact it has on our team.

• Learn a proven process to gain 5 to 15 more hours per week and make your team 35 percent more productive in six months or sooner.

• Understand what stress and urgency addiction does to our decision-making capabilities and how to create a culture of sustainability.

- Learn the Six Stances to quickly shift "energetic posturing" as a leader to increase your influence with your board, clients, prospects, colleagues, direct reports, and employees.

With the ongoing application of your new tools, you'll be able to do the following:

- Shift colleagues, team members, board members, and family members from their Critter State (fight/flight/freeze/faint) into their Smart State (full access to emotions, innovation, and desire for positive outcomes).

- Increase focus and presence to build stronger leadership.

- Communicate more explicitly, resulting in faster, more effective, and complete outcomes.

- Increase transparency through proven accountability structures.

- Build a sustainable culture in which burnout and unvoiced frustrations are a distant memory.

THE NEUROSCIENCE OF INFLUENCE: MARKET BETTER, SELL BETTER, AND LEAD BETTER WITH NEUROSCIENCE

Now more than ever, leaders need to be able to influence outcomes. Real influence is about forging deep connections quickly, stepping into someone's world authentically, and striving for consistent win-win outcomes. In this workshop you'll learn potent neuroscience techniques for getting buy-in, agreement, and enduring loyalty from *anyone*.

You'll accomplish the following:

- Learn to calibrate when someone is in rapport, in their frontal lobes, versus in fear.

- Practice all areas of rapport techniques: physical body, vocal, sensory systems, key words and gestures, and Meta Programs, first in isolation and then together.

- Increase your awareness of the unspoken 93 percent of communication.

- Apply rapport to key client situations and practice needle mover conversations.

- Discover the six most potent Meta Programs that define a human being's world.

- Learn how to communicate to people in their exact Meta Programs to influence, connect, and build deep trust.

- See yourself as an easily predictable leader and see how to change this to get greater performance from your team.

- Witness specific and highly successful applications of these techniques in sales, marketing, and talent and board management and recruiting scenarios.

With the ongoing application of your new tools, you'll be able to accomplish the following:

- Close sales up to 50 percent faster and increase close rate by over 44 percent.

- Deliver marketing messages that are up to 310 percent more effective and increase marketing demand generation by over 300 percent.

- Increase team member emotional engagement, loyalty, and ownership focus 67 to 100 percent.

- Be able to identify the differences between your map and someone else's and how to build bridges that minimize conflict and maximize safety, belonging, and mattering.

THE NEUROSCIENCE OF NAVIGATING CHANGE: MANAGE CHAOS, CLEAR CONFLICT, AND RESOLVE RESISTANCE

Rapid and relentless change is the norm in today's global business environment. How do we rewire the brain to forge positive associations and patterns with change? How do we shift from stress and fear to trust and enthusiasm in change scenarios?

You'll accomplish the following:

- Learn the three Key Change Modalities: Resilience Cycle, Logical Levels of Change, and Present and Desired States.

- Understand the Problem Cycle (how many of us are conditioned to focus on what is *not* working and how we can learn to focus on what we can create).

- Discover the three default roles of Victim, Rescuer, and Persecutor and how to shift our own roles and those of our colleagues, team members, and others to their positive counterpart roles.

- Practice five energy management techniques to increase motivation, enthusiasm, and genuine excitement in the work group.

- Experience giving effective feedback (how and when, including the optimal mindset, scripts and stages, and the essentials to ensure behavior change).

- Discover how to manage conflict (learning what is healthy and what is dysfunctional and understanding the optimal ways of structuring work flow to get and stay healthy).

- Learn how we form habits, release them, and change them (the physiology and the practice of forming new positive habits).

With ongoing application of your new tools, you'll be able to achieve the following:

- Identify the brain-based blocks to change and help team members release them swiftly.

- Build greater communication and trust in change and rapid growth scenarios.

- Add humor and humanity to the change process, enabling empathy, compassion, empowerment, true collaboration, and teamwork.

- Increase team member emotional engagement, loyalty, and ownership focus by 67 to 100 percent.

- Enable individuals to become up to 50 percent more productive.

- Increase revenues and profits by up to 210 percent annually.

- Bring your team the ability to apply our communication techniques and thinking styles both at home and at work, resulting in an increase in personal fulfillment and energy level.

THE NEUROSCIENCE OF OPTIMAL TEAMS: CREATE COLLABORATION, ALIGNMENT, AND COHESION

How do we create teams that feel connection, display accountability, and deliver consistent high-quality results? Would you like to have three people do the work of four to five people?

You'll accomplish the following:

- Learn the seven neuro tools to create profound levels of focus and accountability, effective delegation, clear communication, deep trust, feedback that inspires performance to new levels, and tribal loyalty.

- Discover the three predictors of highly effective and efficient teams—and a framework for identifying and forming the most intelligent teams to raise the organizational IQ.

- See how the brain collaborates and the surprising truth about creating and maintaining emotional alignment and engagement.

- Learn the two essential pathways the brain follows to determine strategy and cause insights.

- Understand metacognition and how "thinking about thinking" can help us solve problems more accurately and quickly and can help us make better decisions faster.

- Learn how to create a code of conduct for powerful teaming and quality outcomes.

- Learn how to foster enthusiasm and momentum via a compelling shared vision.

- Understand connectors within a company and how to create natural teaming and a culture of meritocracy.

With the ongoing application of your new tools, you'll be able to achieve the following:

- Identify optimal team members and give them a framework for collaboration, which will boost overall teamwork and collaboration.

- Form potent team identities to foster loyalty and trust.

- Strategize more effectively and solve problems faster together, causing increased alignment and cohesion.

- Intentionally activate the Reward Network versus the Pain Network to boost performance, loyalty, retention, collaboration, and innovation.

- Increase team member emotional engagement, loyalty, and ownership focus by 67 to 100 percent.

- Enable individuals to become up to 50 percent more productive.

Bring your team the ability to apply our communication techniques and thinking styles both at home and at work, resulting in an increase in personal fulfillment and energy level.

KEYNOTE PROGRAMS

Engage your audience, motivate your employees, and thrill your clients with the programs below or use custom-crafted programs for your specific objective:

Create the Culture of Your Dreams

In this session you'll learn potent neuroscience techniques for creating a culture of passion, growth, commitment, initiative, and resilience. You'll learn the secrets of high-engagement cultures in which employees deliver terrific performance, have balanced lifestyles, and avoid burnout. Want higher employee satisfaction scores, better results, and happier teams? Be sure to request this program.

Guarantee Growth: Leverage Neuroscience for Predictable Revenue, Passionate Teams, and Profitable Growth

In today's uncertain economic climate, you need the latest tools to optimize your growth and employees for profits to soar. Chances are, you're growing in one of these areas but not all three at the same time. What if you could?

Influence Any Outcome: Use Neuroscience to Sell Better, Lead Better, and Market Better

Influence is no longer about doing something to someone to get what you want. Real influence is about forging deep connections quickly, stepping into someone's world authentically, and striving for consistent win-win outcomes.

Make Your Team Smarter Overnight: The Neuroscience of Compelling Leadership

Today's leaders need to exhibit a deeper ability to communicate and influence others to cause higher levels of accountability and productivity on their teams.

Quota Busters: Get Inside the Brain of Your Buyers

In this highly interactive training, we explore aspects of neuroscience that can be applied to sales with rapid results. Participants will be able to deeply understand their buyers and experience a shift in their relationship to prospecting, marketing, lead generation and cultivation, and client care.

Strategic and Team Building Retreats

Tell us your vision, and we'll create it together. Contact us at any of the following:

Phone: 415-320-6580

Website: www.SmartTribesInstitute.com

Twitter: @comaford

LinkedIn: www.linkedin.com/in/comaford

Facebook: www.facebook.com/comaford

SmartTribe Twitter community: #SmartTribes

Let's keep fostering emotional resilience in a world where change is constant. Together, we can help our teams learn to love change and thrive in it.

Here's to powering your tribe!

Notes

Preface

1. To access our complimentary growth assessment and leadership assessment tools, visit SmartTribesInstitute.com.
2. Christine Comaford, *SmartTribes: How Teams Become Brilliant Together* (Portfolio /Penguin, New York, 2013).
3. Daniel Goleman, *Emotional Intelligence* (Random House, New York, 2012).

Chapter 1

1. Wayne Dyer, "Success Secrets," Wayne's blog, *Dr. Wayne W. Dyer*, http://www .drwaynedyer.com/blog/success-secrets/, accessed May 2, 2017.
2. Key texts by Gregory Bateson are *Steps to an Ecology of Mind* (University of Chicago Press, Chicago, 2000) and *Mind and Nature: A Necessary Unity* (Hampton Press, New York, 2002). To learn more about Bateson, see his biography at http://www.intercul turalstudies.org/Bateson/biography.html or https://en.wikipedia.org/wiki/Gregory _Bateson.
3. For a comprehensive review of Paul D. MacLean's work, see his 1990 book *The Triune Brain in Evolution* (Plenum Press, New York).
4. Find out more about Carl Buchheit's transformative neuro-linguistic programming (NLP) techniques at http://nlpmarin.com/.

Chapter 2

1. Abraham Maslow, "A Theory of Human Motivation," *Psychological Review*, vol. 50 (1943): 370–396.
2. Susan Greenfield, *Mind Change: How Digital Technologies Are Leaving Their Mark on Our Brains* (Random House, New York, 2015). Also see http://www.susangreenfield .com/.
3. Carla J. Shatz, "The Developing Brain," *Scientific American* (1992): 60–67. For more information about Carla Shatz's work, see http://web.stanford.edu/group/shatzlab/.
4. Donald O. Hebb, *The Organization of Behavior: A Neuropsychological Theory* (Laurence Erlbaum Associates, Mahwah, NJ, 2002).

Chapter 3

1. Travis Bradberry, *Emotional Intelligence 2.0* (TalentSmart, San Diego, 2009), p. 14.

Chapter 4

1. Wilhelm Reich, *Character-Analysis: Principles and Technique for Psychoanalysts in Practice and in Training*, translated by Theodore P. Wolfe (Orgone Institute Press, New York, 1945).

2. Carl Buchheit, "10 Delusions of Personal Growth," http://ezinearticles.com/?10 -Delusions-of-Personal-Growth&id=2676253.

3. See Richard Bandler and John Grinder, *The Structure of Magic: A Book About Language and Therapy*, vol. 1 (Science and Behavior Books, Mountain View, CA, 1975); Richard Bandler and John Grinder, *The Structure of Magic: A Book About Communication and Change*, vol. 2 (Science and Behavior Books, Mountain View, CA, 1975); Richard Bandler and John Grinder, *Frogs into Princes* (Real People Press, Boulder, CO, 1979); and Richard Bandler, John Grinder, and Virginia Satir, *Changing with Families: A Book About Further Education for Being Human* (Science and Behavior Books, Mountain View, CA, 1976).

4. For example, see Madhav Goyal, Sonal Singh, and Erica Sibinga, "Meditation Programs for Psychological Stress and Well-Being: A Systematic Review and Meta-Analysis," *JAMA Internal Medicine*, vol. 174, no. 3 (2014): 357–368; also available at http:// jamanetwork.com/journals/jamainternalmedicine/fullarticle/1809754. Neal Conan, "Author Interview: Neurotheology: This Is Your Brain on Religion," *Talk of the Nation*, NPR (website), December 15, 2010, http://www.npr.org/2010/12/15/132078267 /neurotheology-where-religion-and-science-collide, accessed May 4, 2017. See also the research of neurotheologist Dr. Andrew Newberg at http://www.andrewnewberg .com/research/.

   Sue McGreevey, "Eight Weeks to a Better Brain: Meditation Study Shows Changes Associated with Awareness, Stress," *Harvard Gazette*, January 21, 2011, http://news.harvard.edu/gazette/story/2011/01/eight-weeks-to-a-better-brain/, accessed May 4, 2017. Britta K. Hölzel, James Carmody, Mark Vangel, et al., "Mindfulness Practice Leads to Increases in Regional Brain Gray Matter Density," *Psychiatry Research: Neuroimaging*, vol. 191, no. 1 (2011): 36–43, http://www.sciencedirect.com /science/article/pii/S092549271000288X, accessed May 4, 2017.

   Kaitlin McLean, "The Healing Art of Meditation," *Yale Scientific*, May 10, 2012, http://www.yalescientific.org/2012/05/the-healing-art-of-meditation/, accessed May 4, 2017. See also the research of neurotheologist Dr. Andrew Newberg at http:// www.andrewnewberg.com/research/.

5. Julia Griffin, "Getting in the Gap: Interview with Wayne Dyer," *One True Self* (website), September 8, 2015, http://onetrueself.com/gap-interview-wayne-dyer/, accessed May 4, 2017.

Chapter 5

1. See https://hbr.org/2012/12/your-companys-history-as-a-leadership-tool. Also see https://hbr.org/2005/01/whats-your-story.

2. For more about the Tension and Empowerment Triangles, see *SmartTribes*, Chapter 8, "Sustainable Results."

3. Chris Koke, "Marines Singing *Frozen*—Let It Go in HD," YouTube, https://www
   .youtube.com/watch?v=nWnGwj9s-Fk, accessed April 24, 2017.
4. Mark Twain, *Following the Equator: A Journey Around the World* (American Publishing
   Company, Hartford, CT, 1897; reprint Jungle Land Publishing (CreateSpace Independent Publishing Platform, Amazon.com, 2016), p. 81.
5. Adaddpted from Scott Sims, "A Four-Step Process for Creating Compelling Content
   for Your Audience," Marketing Profs, February 8, 2016, http://www.marketingprofs
   .com/articles/2016/29307/a-four-step-process-for-creating-compelling-content-for
   -your-audience, accessed May 5, 2017. Sims cites Alex Williams as the original creator
   of the CURVE method, originally developed for e-mail subject lines: Alex Williams,
   "The CURVE Method for Engaging Email Subject Lines," *Modern Marketing Blog*, Or-
   acle Marketing Cloud, February 7, 2014, https://blogs.oracle.com/marketingcloud
   /curve-email-2, accessed May 5, 2017.

Chapter 6
1. For a more in-depth discussion of the Outcome Frame, see Chapter 6 in *SmartTribes* or
   see it demonstrated here: www.SmartTribesInstitute.com/vision.
2. For a Leadership Levels template, please see www.SmartTribesInstitute.com/STP.

Chapter 7
1. For additional tools to create a "same-as experience" with others, see Chapter 6 in
   SmartTribes.
2. Paul Tosey and Jane Mathison, *Introducing Neuro-Linguistic Programming*, Centre for
   Management Learning & Development, School of Management, University of Surrey,
   2006, http://www.som.surrey.ac.uk/NLP/Resources/IntroducingNLP.pdf, accessed
   May 10, 2017.
3. See Chapter 8 of *SmartTribes* for more about shifting from victim, rescuer, and persecutor to the empowering alternative.

Chapter 8
1. *Steve Jobs: The Lost Interview*, Magnolia Pictures, 1995, available at http://www.mag
   pictures.com/stevejobsthelostinterview/.
2. See Scott Horton's unconscious bias exercise at https://www.youtube.com/watch
   ?v=i_52T8ufdZM.
3. Vernā Myers, *Moving Diversity Forward: How to Go from Well-Meaning to Well-Doing*
   (American Bar Association, Chicago, 2011). Also see http://vernamyers.com/.
4. *ScienceDaily*, "How Stress Tears Us Apart: Enzyme Attacks Synaptic Molecule, Leading to
   Cognitive Impairment," September 18, 2014, https://www.sciencedaily.com/releases
   /2014/09/140918091418.htm, accessed May 8, 2017;

   "What Causes Depression? Onset of Depression More Complex Than a Chem-
   ical Imbalance," Harvard Health Publications, Harvard Medical School, April 11,
   2017, http://www.health.harvard.edu/mind-and-mood/what-causes-depression, accessed May 8, 2017; and "Stress," Medical Reference Guide, University of Maryland

Medical Center, http://www.umm.edu/health/medical/reports/articles/stress, accessed May 8, 2017.

5. As quoted in Salim Ismail, *Exponential Organizations: Why New Organizations Are Ten Times Better, Faster, and Cheaper Than Yours (and What to Do About It)* (Diversion Books, New York, 2014); and "List of Cognitive Biases," *Wikipedia: The Free Encyclopedia,* https://en.wikipedia.org/wiki/List_of_cognitive_biases, accessed May 8, 2017.

6. Christine Ann Lawson, *Understanding the Borderline Mother: Helping Her Children Transcend the Intense, Unpredictable, and Volatile Relationship* (Rowman & Littlefield, Lanham, MD, 2004).

7. Adapted from Lawson, *Understanding the Borderline Mother.*

8. Find out more about Carl Buchheit's transformative neuro-linguistic programming (NLP) techniques at http://nlpmarin.com/.

9. For more about the Anthropologist stance, see Chapter 6 in *SmartTribes.*

10. Keith Ferrazzi, "Seven Ways to Improve Employee Development Programs," *Harvard Business Review,* July 31, 2015, https://hbr.org/2015/07/7-ways-to-improve-employee-development-programs.

11. See the website https://management30.com/practice/merit-money/.

Chapter 9

1. Bert Hellinger, *Love's Hidden Symmetry: What Makes Love Work in Relationships* (Zeig, Tucker & Theisen, Phoenix, AZ, 1998). See also http://www.hellingerpa.com/constellation.shtml.

Chapter 10

1. Judith Lynn Fisher-Blando, *Workplace Bullying: Aggressive Behavior and Its Effect on Job Satisfaction and Productivity,* dissertation, University of Phoenix, February 2008, http://www.workplaceviolence911.com/docs/20081215.pdf, accessed May 8, 2017.

2. For more about the Tension and Empowerment Triangles, see Chapter 8 of *SmartTribes.*

Chapter 13

1. Christine Comaford, "Why Smart People Make Stupid Decisions," *Forbes,* March 11, 2017, https://www.forbes.com/sites/christinecomaford/2017/03/11/why-smart-people-make-stupid-decisions/#2082fc445405, accessed May 8, 2017.

Index

influencing phrases for, 98–99
mind management and, 7–10, 15
Smart and, 79, 97, 136
Cultural GAME Plan, 133, 149–154
Curiosity, 40, 74, 79, 148
CURVE model, 74
Cytokines, brain and, 24–25

D

Data, types of, 10–15, 84
Decoder
  Borderline Behavior, 145–146
  Distorted Thinking, 66, 70–71
  Organismic Rights, 49–51
  SBM Behavior, 96–97
Defining Personal Values kit, 202
Desire, 35, 198
Desired State (DS)
  through belonging, 21–23
  creating, 90
  human craving and, 18
  Outcome Frame and, 41–42, 91
  VAK anchoring and, 85
Diagnostic and Statistical Manual of
    Mental Disorders (DSM), 141
Direction, Toward-Away, 106, 107–108
Distorted Thinking Decoder, 66, 70–71
Diversity, 136–138, 203, 207
Diversity, Equity and Inclusion Structures,
    138, 207
Dopamine, 72, 149, 150
DS. *See* Desired State
DSM. *See* Diagnostic and Statistical
    Manual of Mental Disorders
Dyer, Wayne, 5, 55, 58

E

Effective Meeting Process, 91, 186, 187
Efficacy, of story, 74
Einstein, Albert, 159, 165–166, 167
Emotion
  energy of, 36–39
  Maneuvers of Consciousness and, 32
  navigating, xvi

power over experiences and, 16
shifting, xiv–xv, xvii, 32–33
in story, 72, 76
wheel, 32, 33–34, 36–37
Emotional agility
  defined, xix
  power equals tools plus, xx–xxi, 26–27
  with Resilience Cycle, xix, xx
  role of, xvi–xix, xviii
Emotional Intelligence (Goleman), xvii
Emotional Intelligence 2.0 (Bradberry), 36
Empowerment, xiv, 71, 185
Empowerment Triangle, 71
Enabling system, with bullying behavior
  ending, 182–185
  tension chart, 183–184
Energetic weight
  as art of showing up, 159–164
  defined, 173–174
  family business and, 206, 207
  quiz, 161–162
Energy
  of consent, 35–36, 38, 42
  of emotion, 36–39
  Relationship Bubble and, 163–164
Energy Recall, 163–164, 174
Engagement, 149, 150, 152, 195. *See also*
    Enroll and engage others
Enroll and engage others. *See also* Meta
    Programs
  Resilience Cycle, 93
  with safety, belonging and mattering,
    95–103
Equity. *See* Diversity, Equity and Inclusion
    Structures
Exodus, of staff, 189–190, 201
Experience, 10–13, 16. *See also* Human
    experience
External soundtrack, 12

F

Family business, board dysfunction and,
    203–207
Feedback, 168–173, 193, 195

About the Author

Bill Gates calls her "super high bandwidth." Bill Clinton has thanked her for "fostering American entrepreneurship."

For over 30 years, human behavior expert, serial entrepreneur, and *New York Times* bestselling author Christine Comaford has helped 700 of the Fortune 1000 and 300 midsize businesses navigate growth and change.

Christine is sought after for the potent neuroscience techniques she teaches that are easy to learn and immediately applicable to real-world challenges. She is known for helping clients optimize growth, enroll and align teams in times of change, and profoundly increase sales, product offerings, and company value. Her coaching, consulting, and strategies have created billions of dollars in new revenue and company value for her clients.

As an entrepreneur, she has built and sold five of her own businesses with an average of 700 percent return on investment. She has served as a board director or board advisor to 36 startups and has invested in over 200 startups (including Google), repeatedly identifying and championing key trends and technologies years before market acceptance, due in part to her work as a software engineer in the early days of Microsoft, Apple, and Adobe.

Christine has consulted to the White House (Clinton and Bush). She was named one of the Top 50 Human Behavior Experts to Follow in 2017 and one of the Global Employee Engagement Influencers in 2017. A leadership columnist for www.Forbes.com and guest lecturer at Harvard Business School, she has appeared on CNN, CNBC, MSNBC, Fox Business Network, *Good Morning America*, and PBS. Stanford Graduate School of Business has done two case studies on her unconventional rise to success as a woman with neither a high school diploma nor a college degree.

Christine believes we can do well and do good, using business as a path for personal development, wealth creation, and philanthropy.

Her two *New York Times* bestselling business books are *SmartTribes: How Teams Become Brilliant Together* and *Rules for Renegades: How to Make More Money, Rock Your Career, and Revel in Your Individuality.*

Connect with Christine:

Free webinars and resources: www.SmartTribesInstitute.com/join

SmartTribes Twitter community: #SmartTribes and #PowerYourTribe

Twitter: @comaford

LinkedIn: www.linkedin.com/in/comaford

Facebook: www.facebook.com/comaford

Websites: www.SmartTribesInstitute.com and PowerYourTribe.com

Wikipedia: https://en.wikipedia.org/wiki/Christine_Comaford